ANIME COLORING BOOK

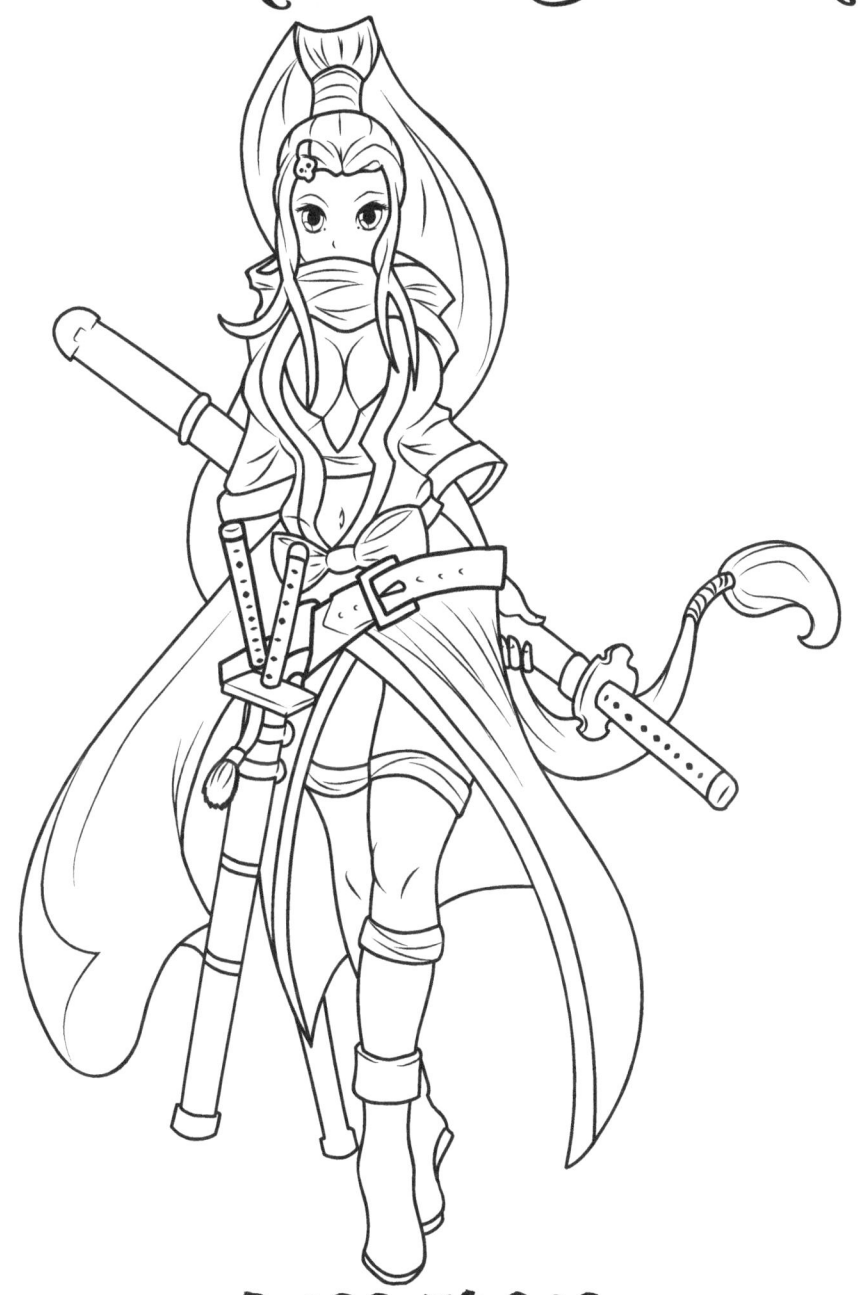

– RUSS FOCUS –

ISBN-13: 978-1720974734   ISBN-10: 172097473X

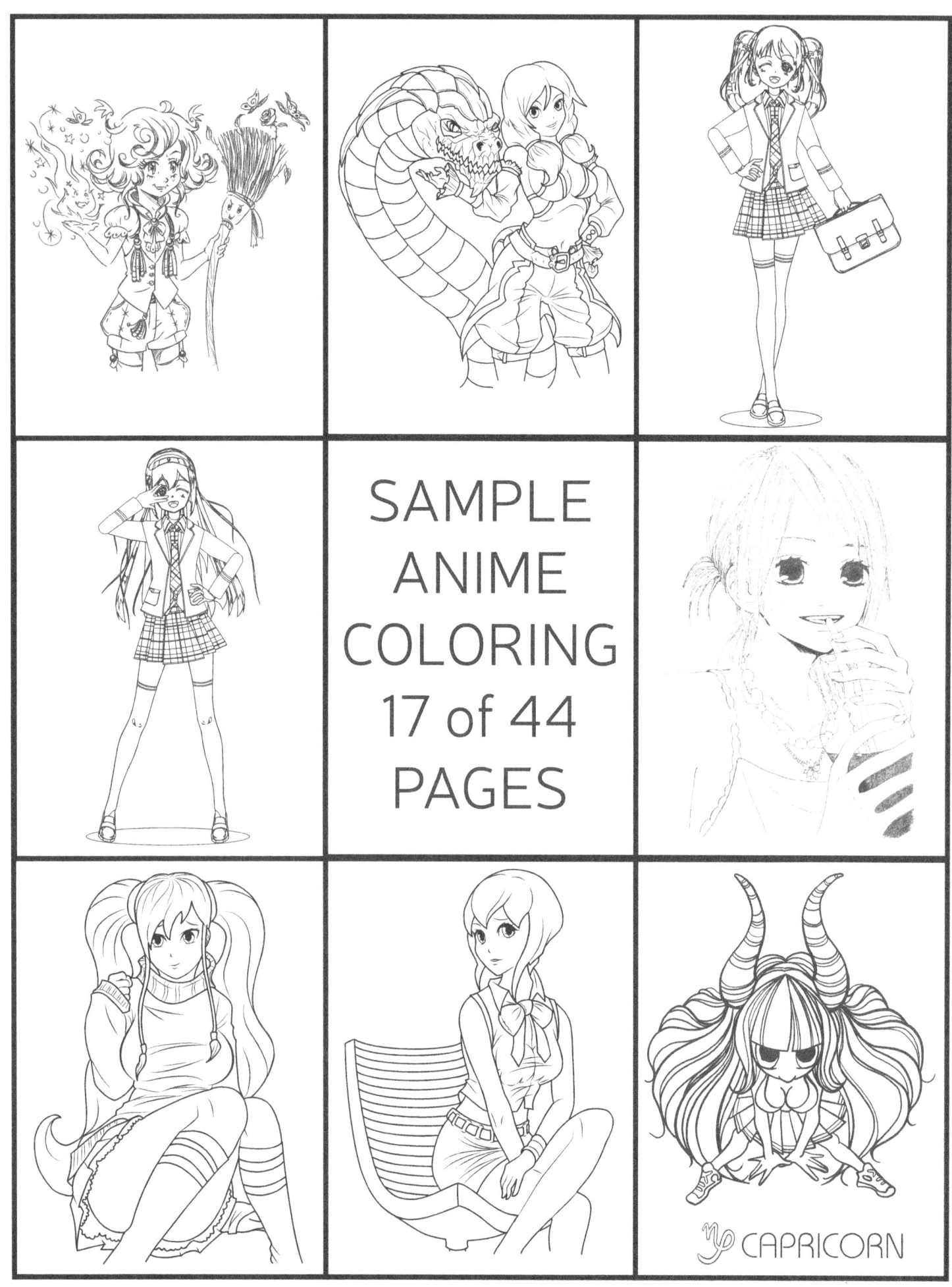

SAMPLE
ANIME
COLORING
17 of 44
PAGES

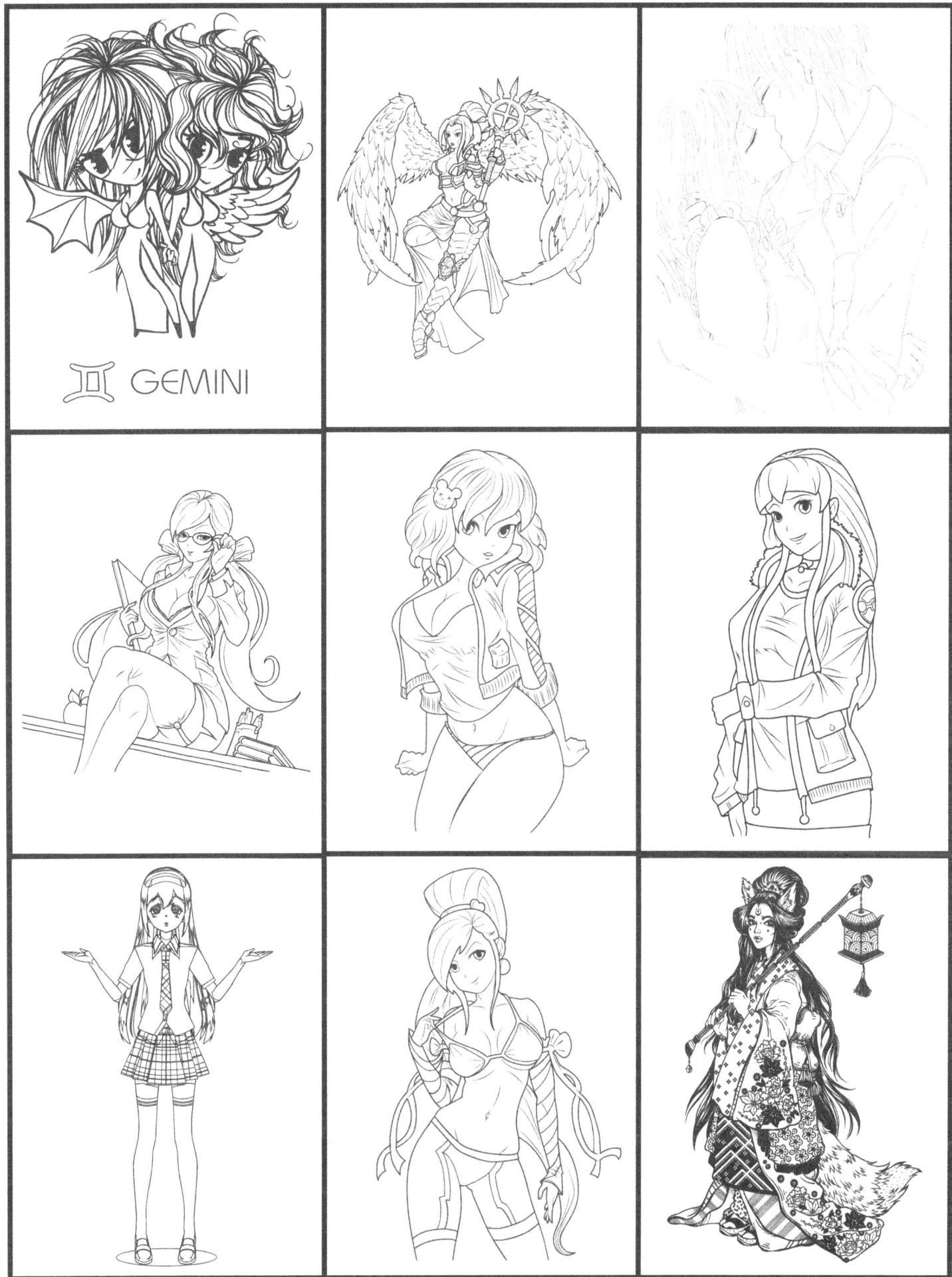

GEMINI

Adorable Manga and Anime Characters set on Anime

www.russfocus.com

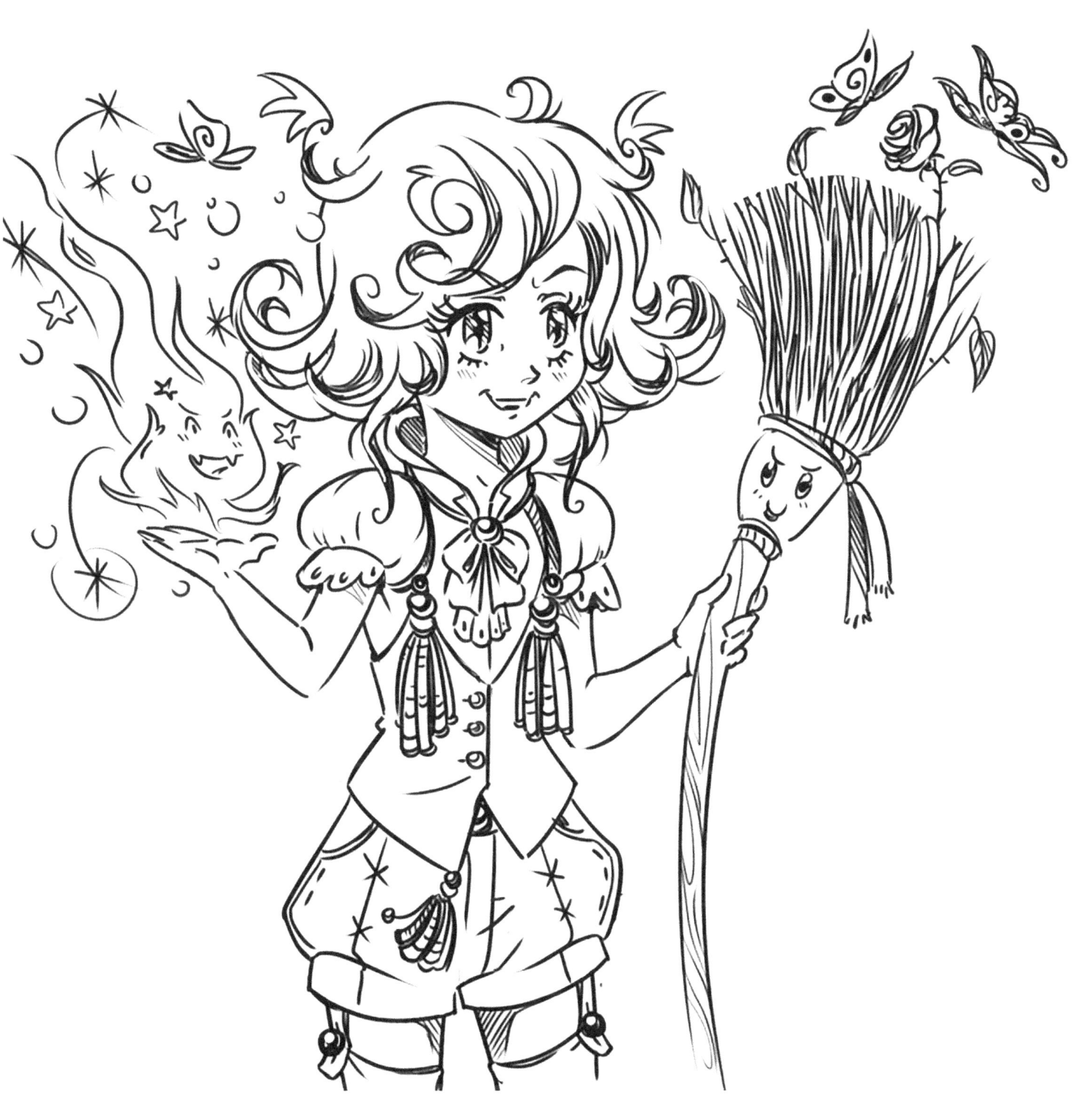

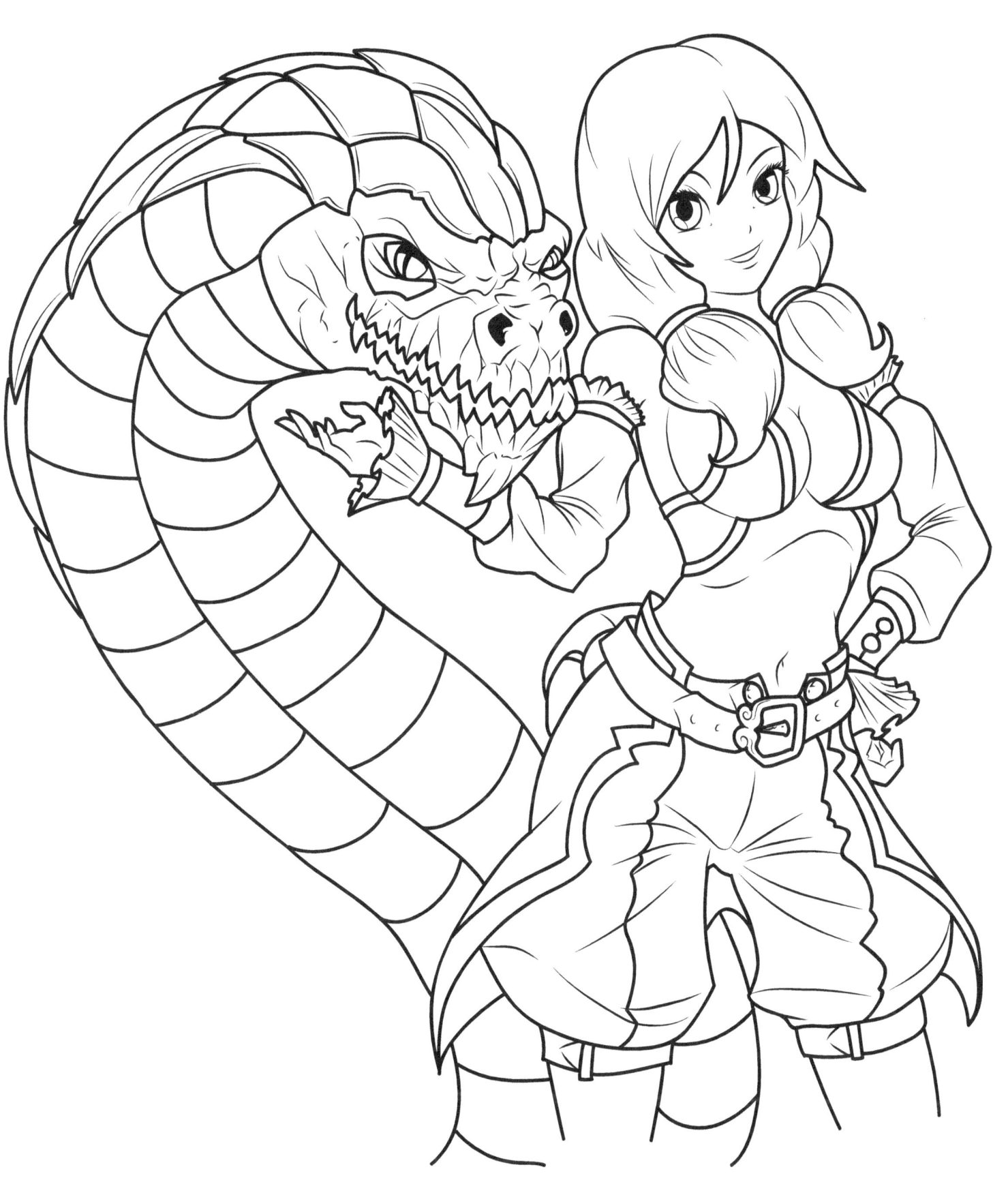

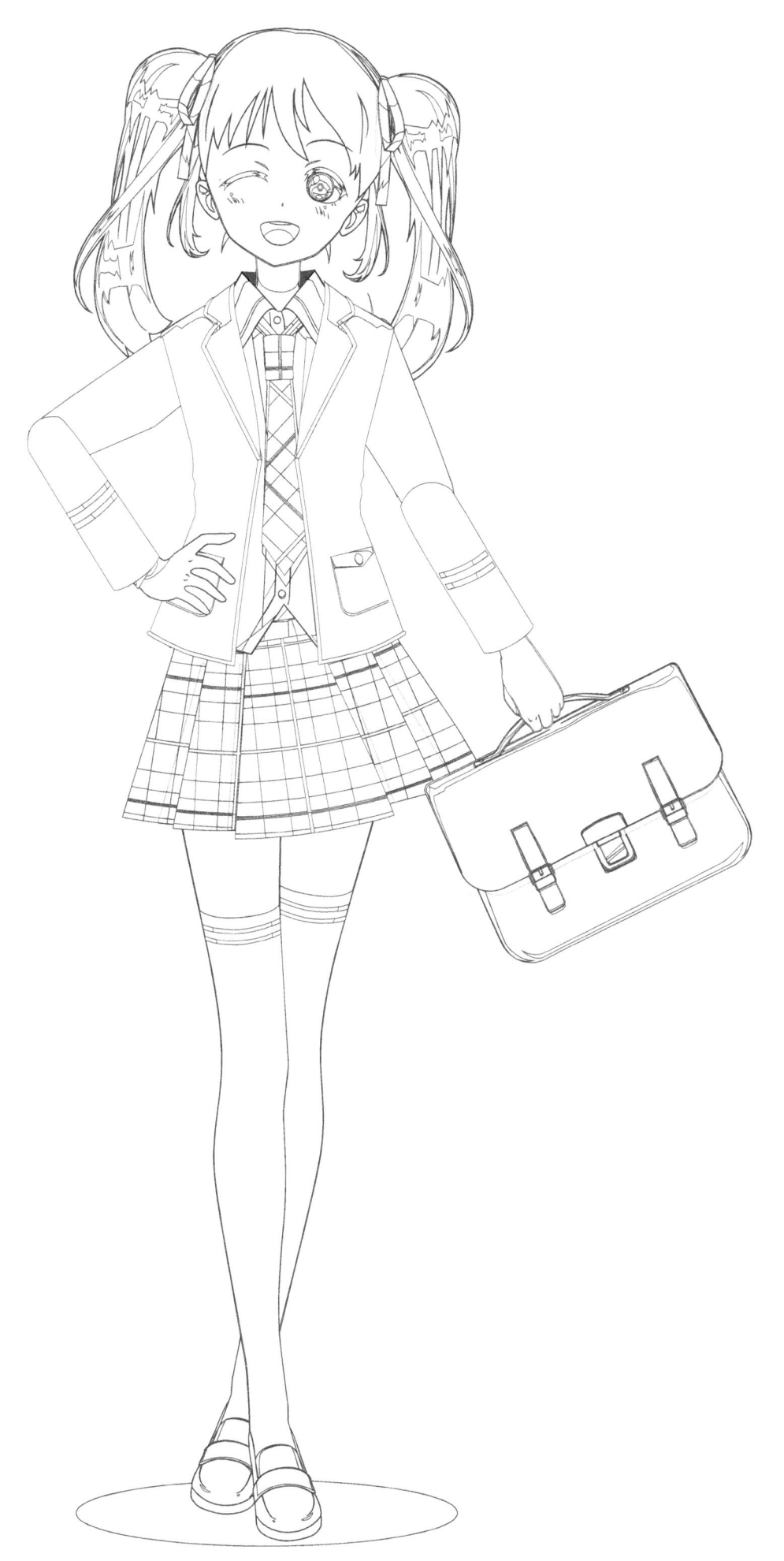

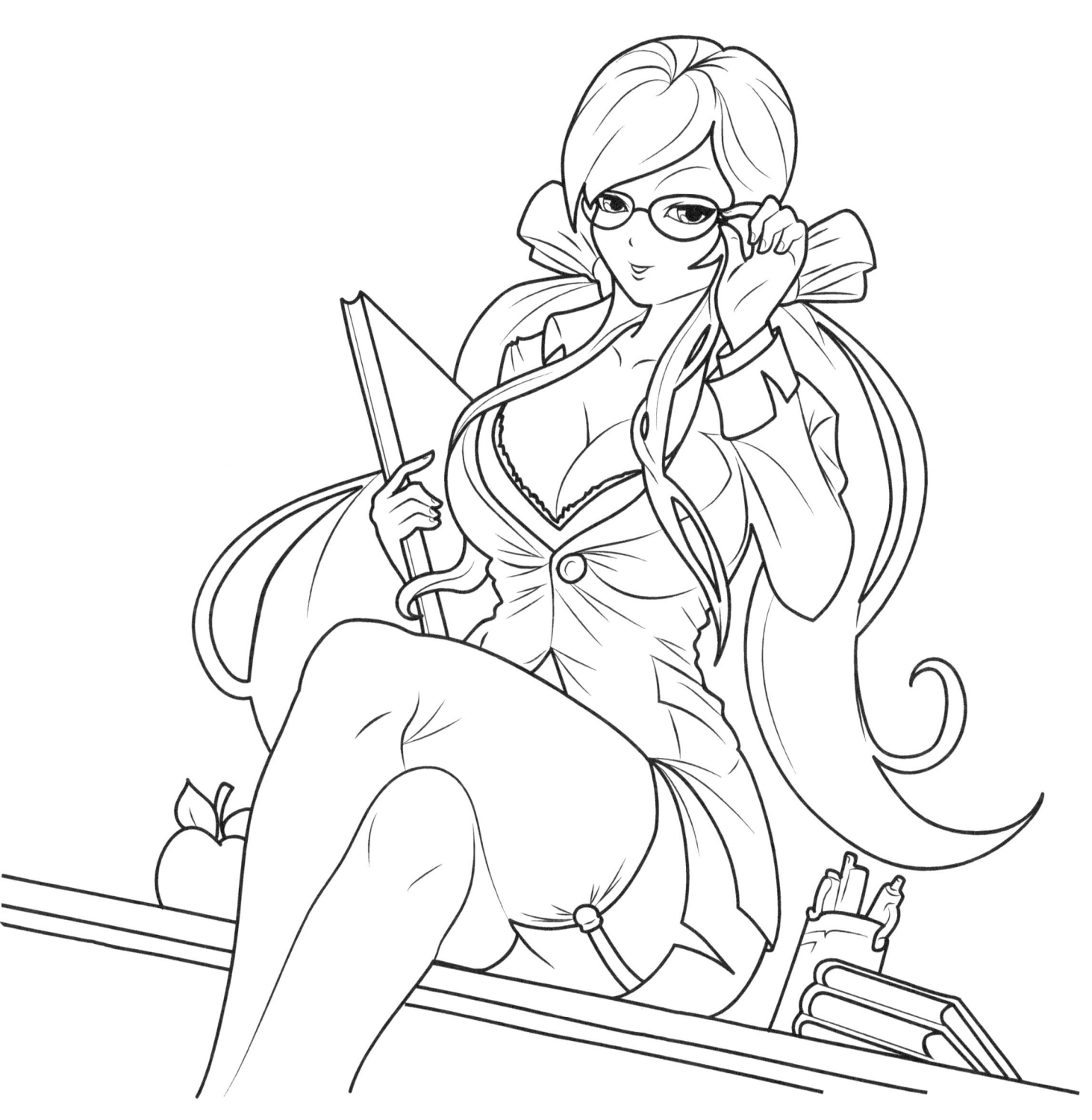

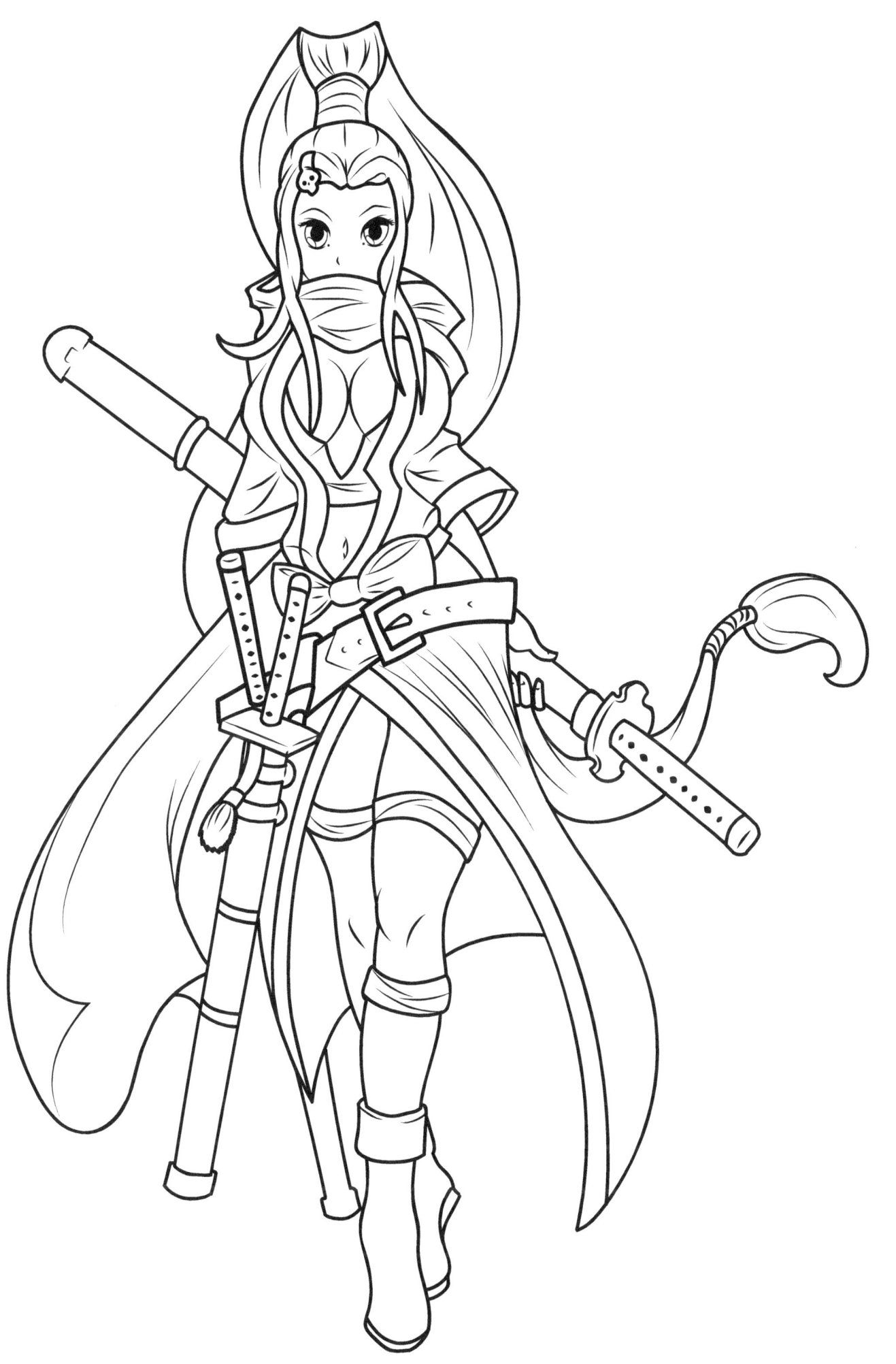

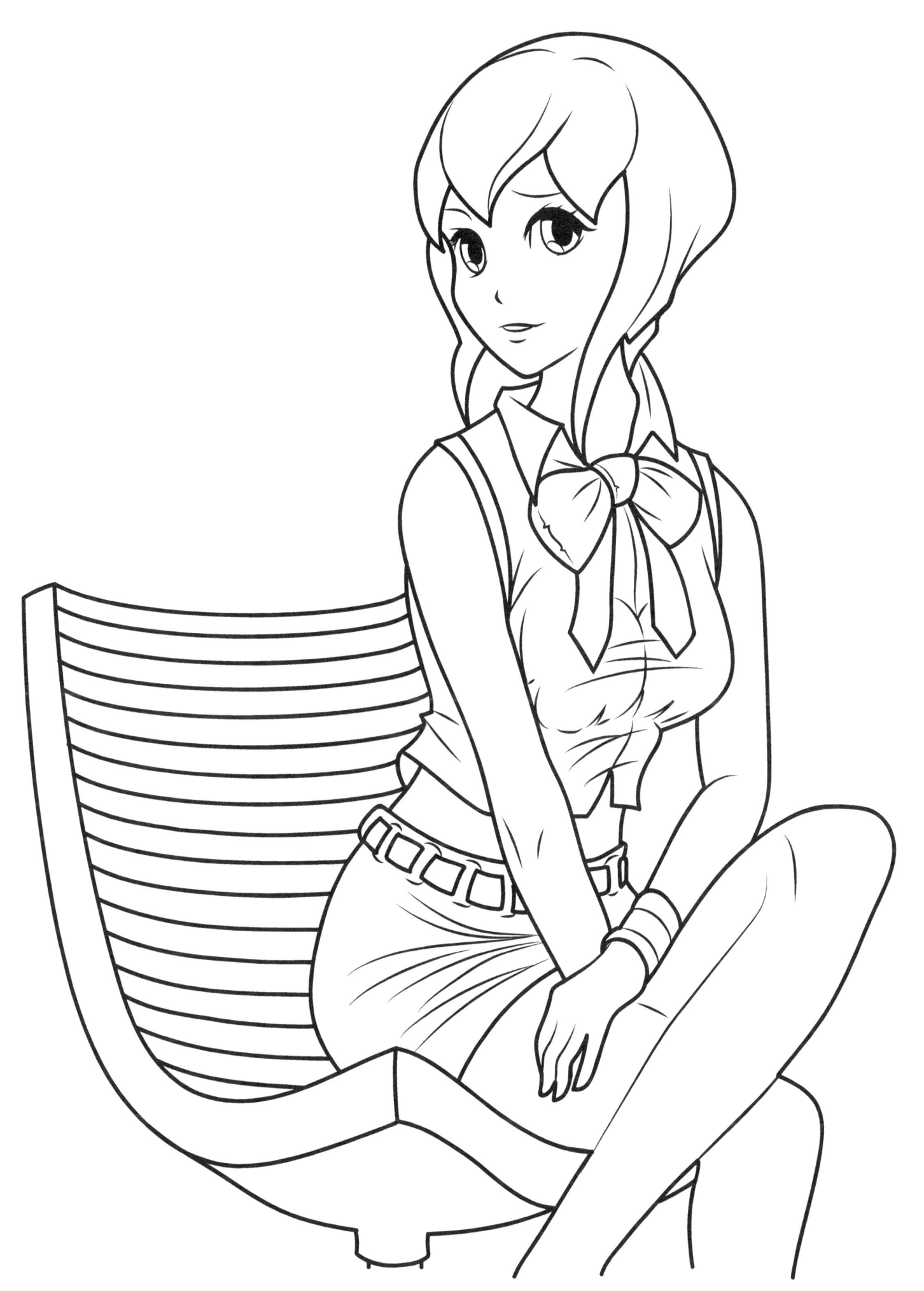

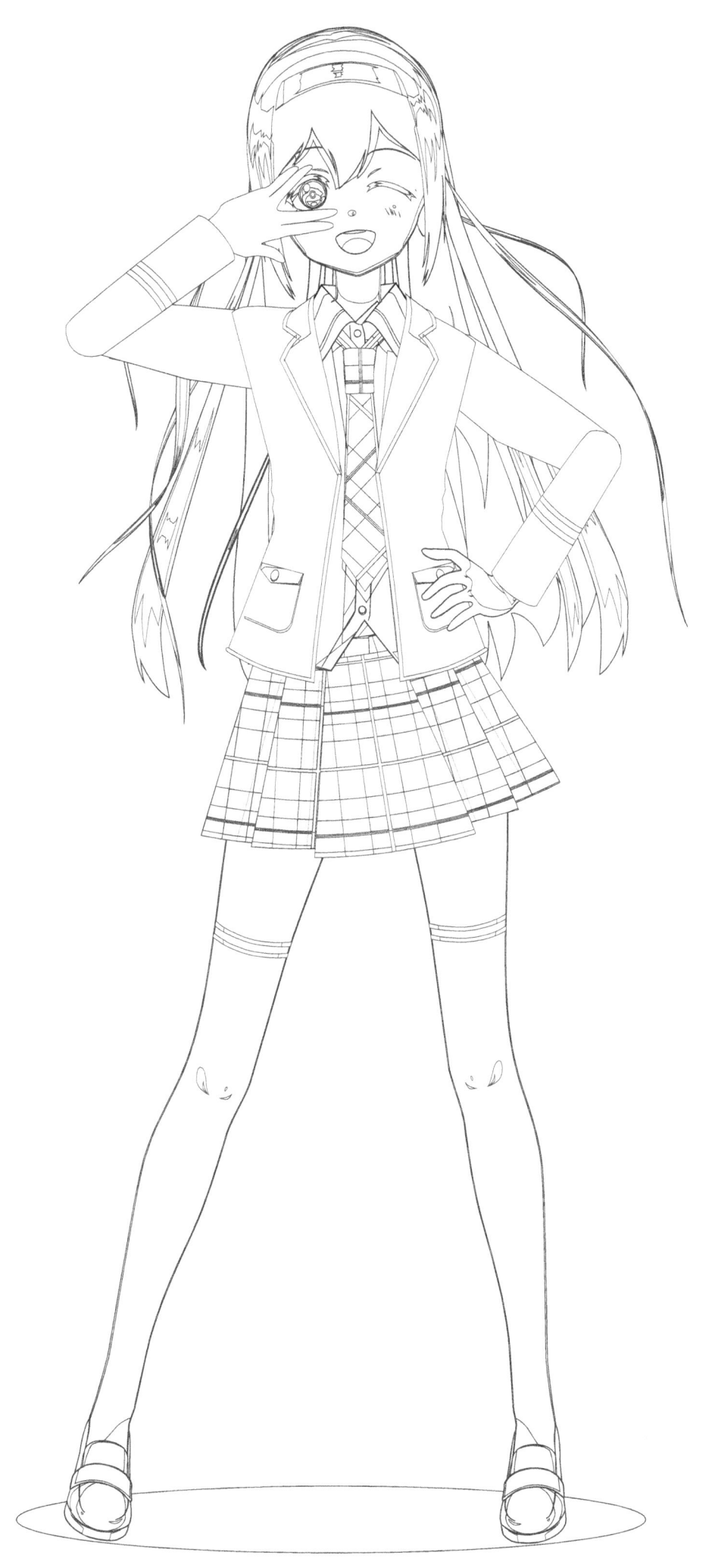

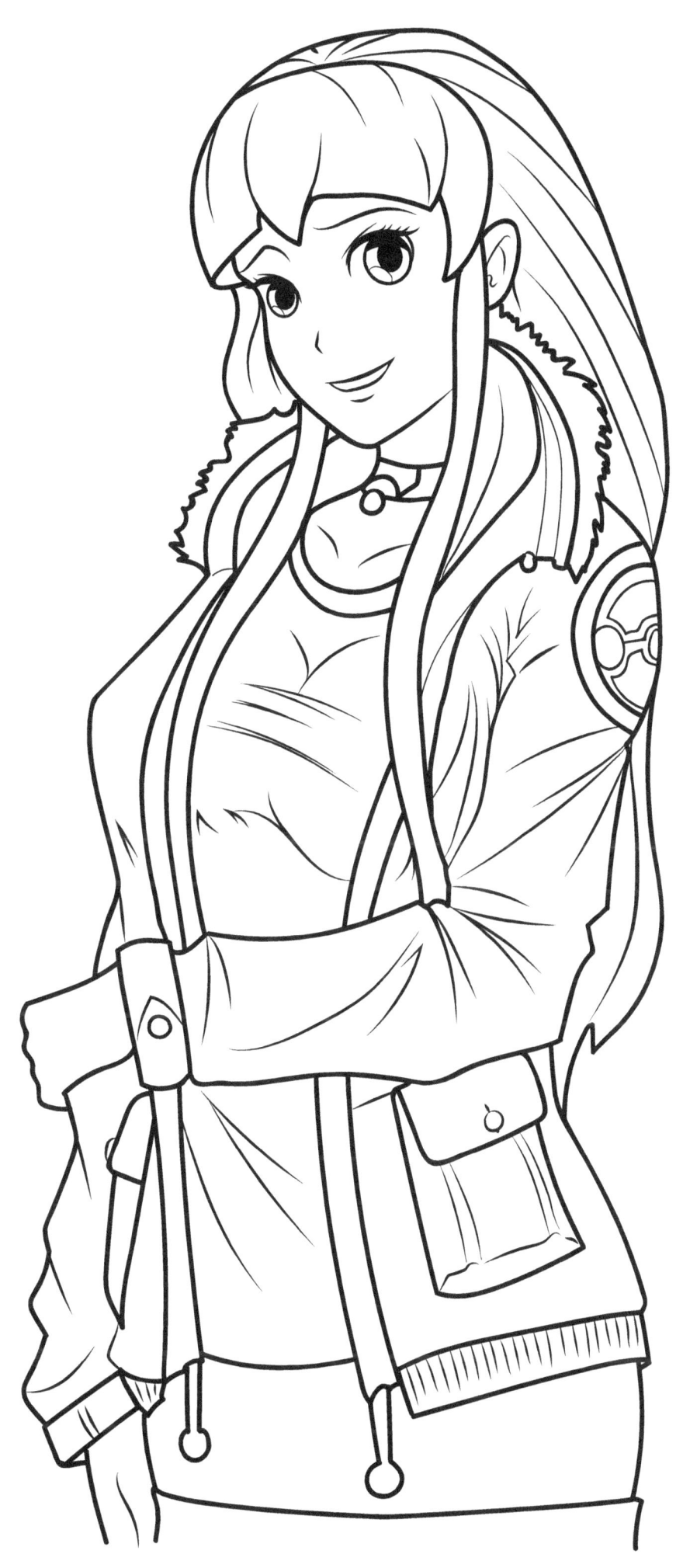

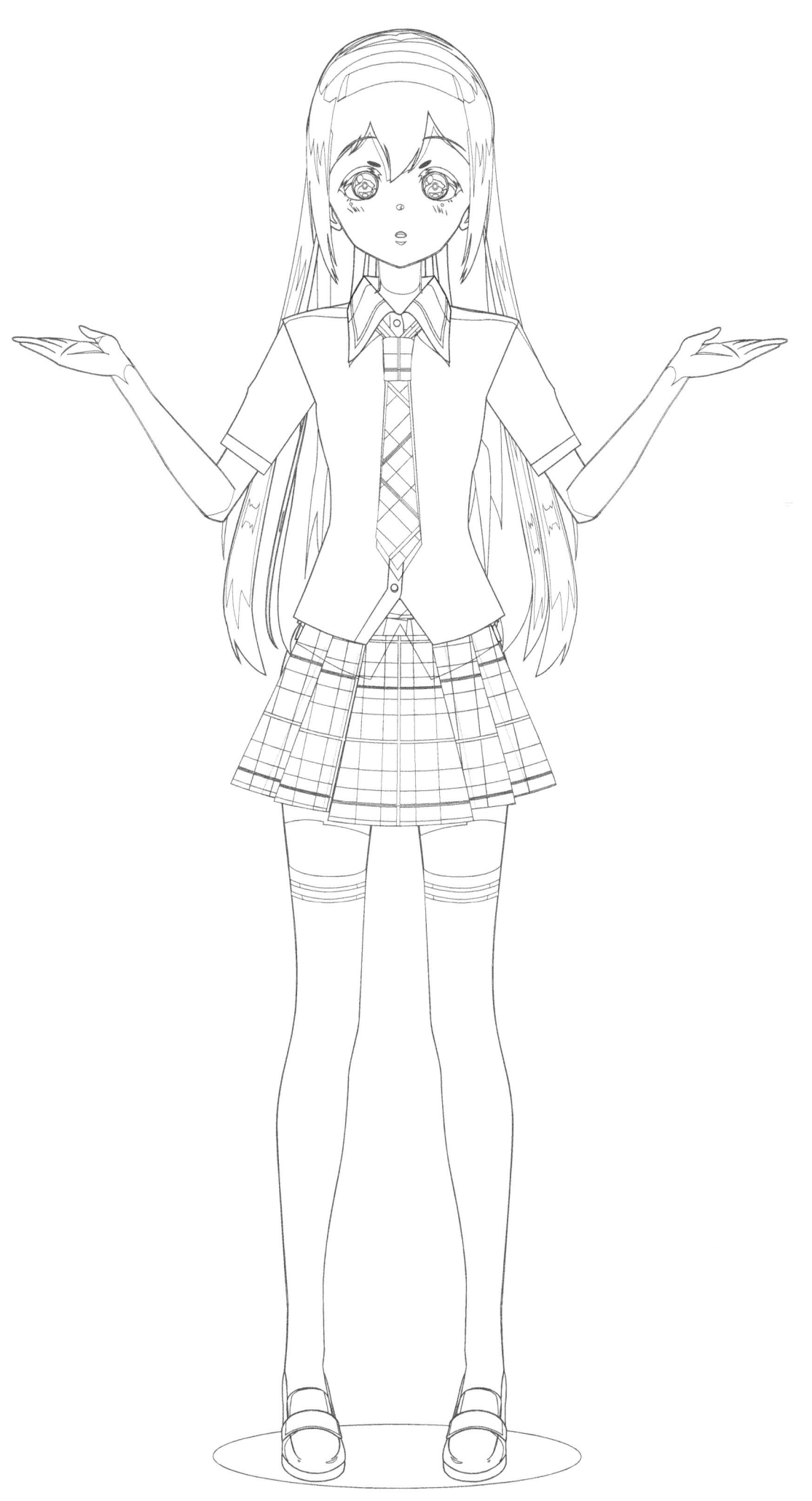

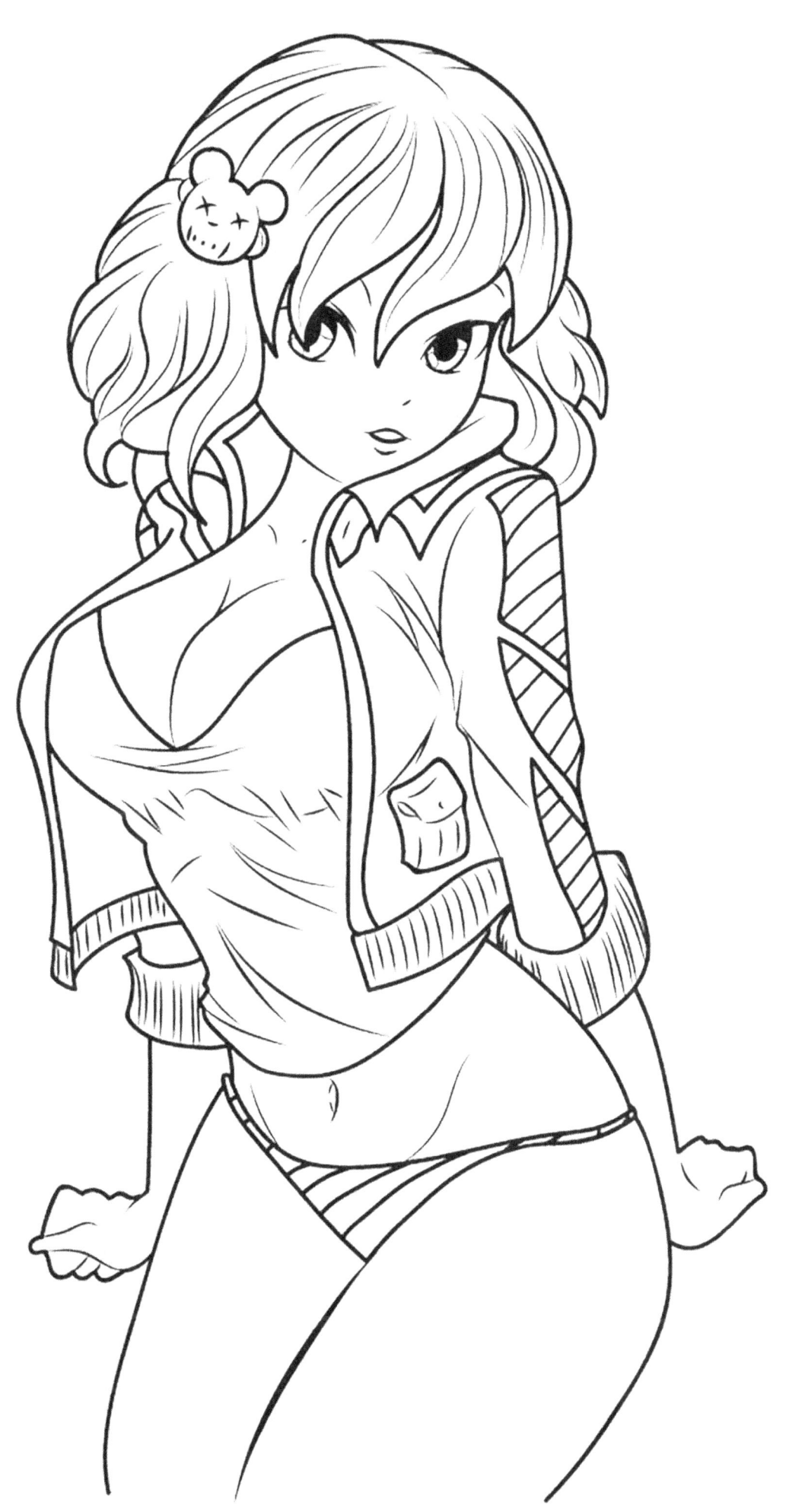

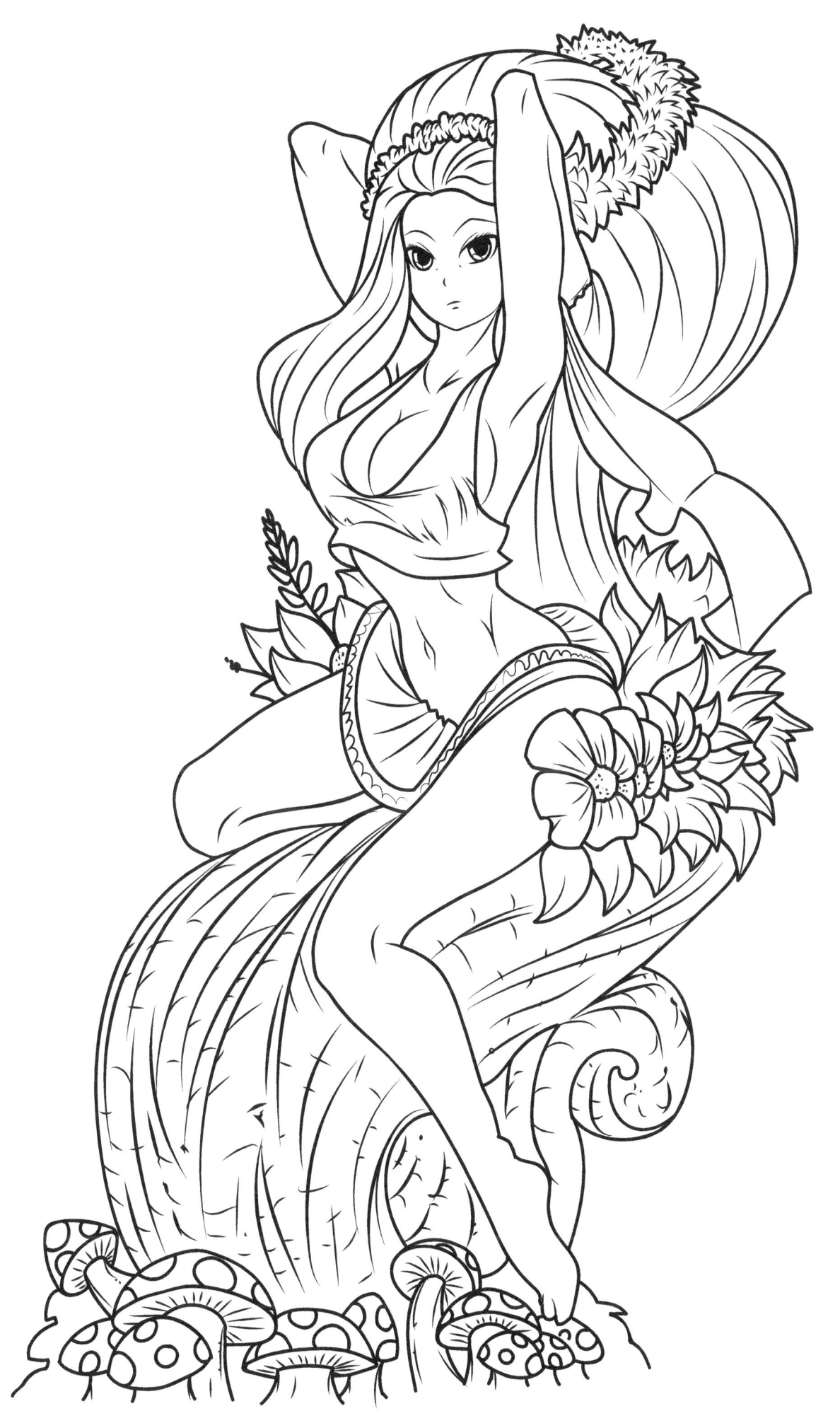

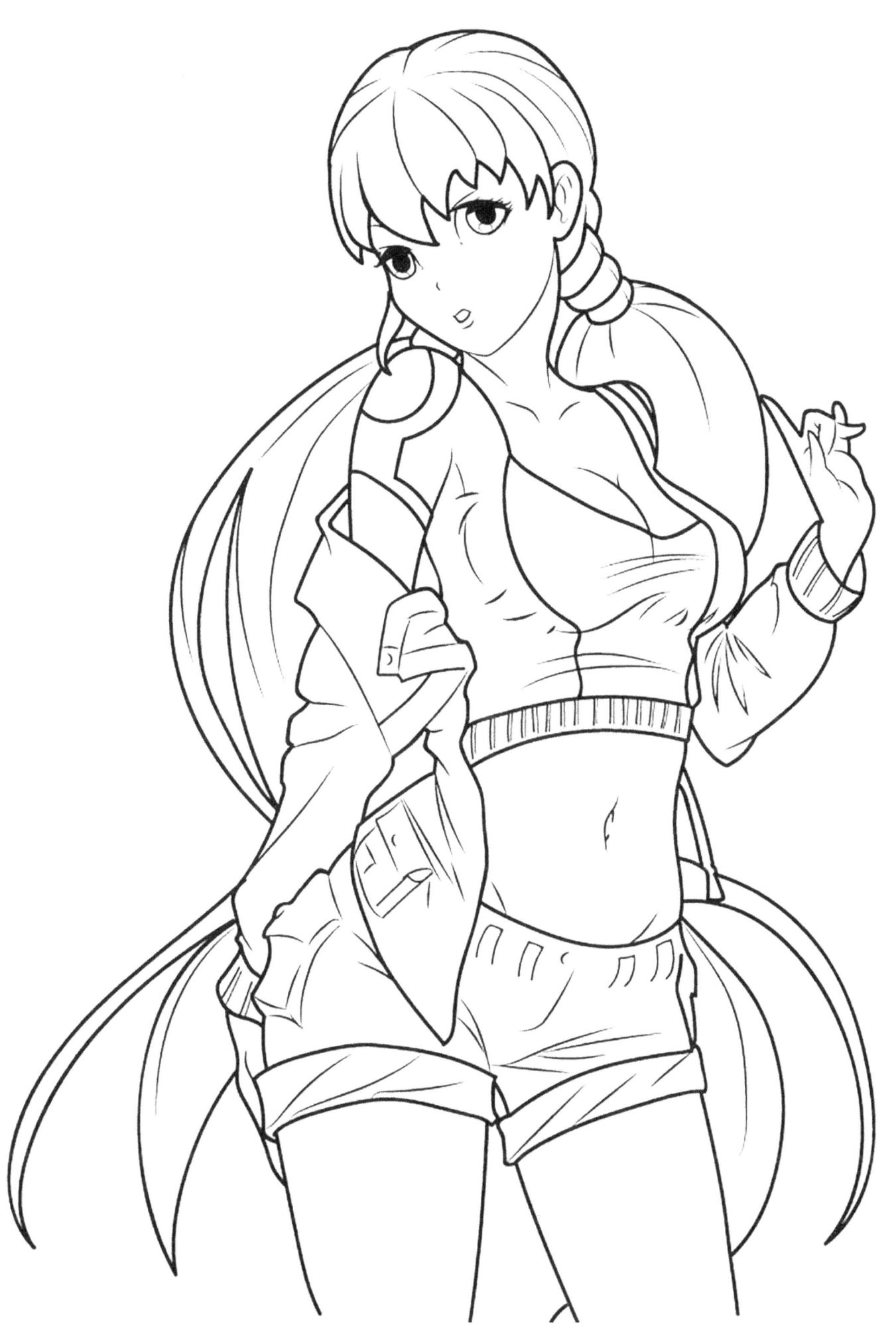

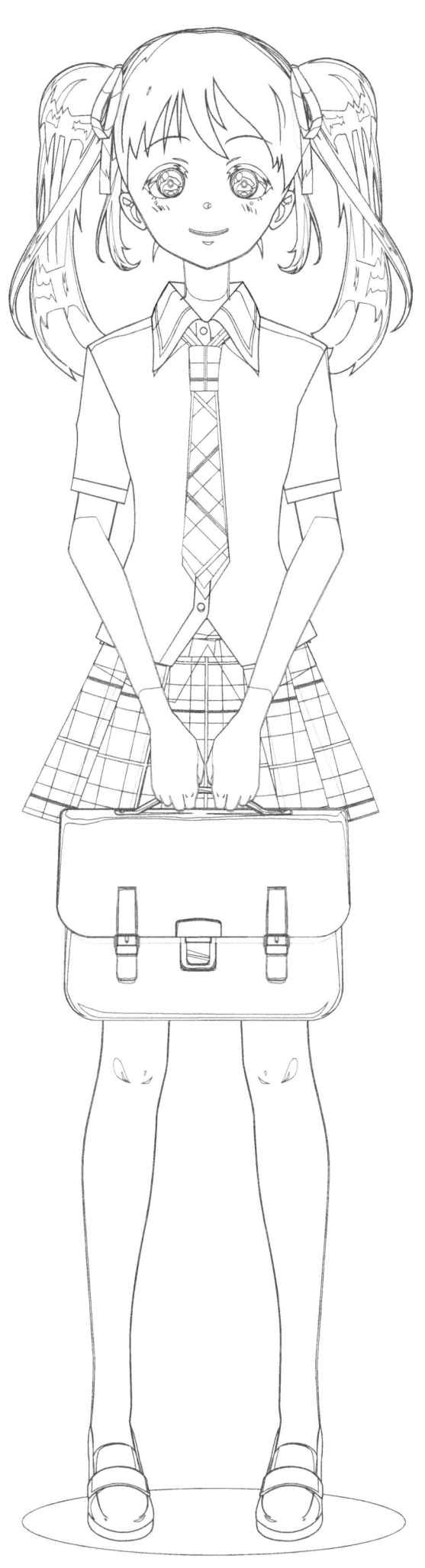

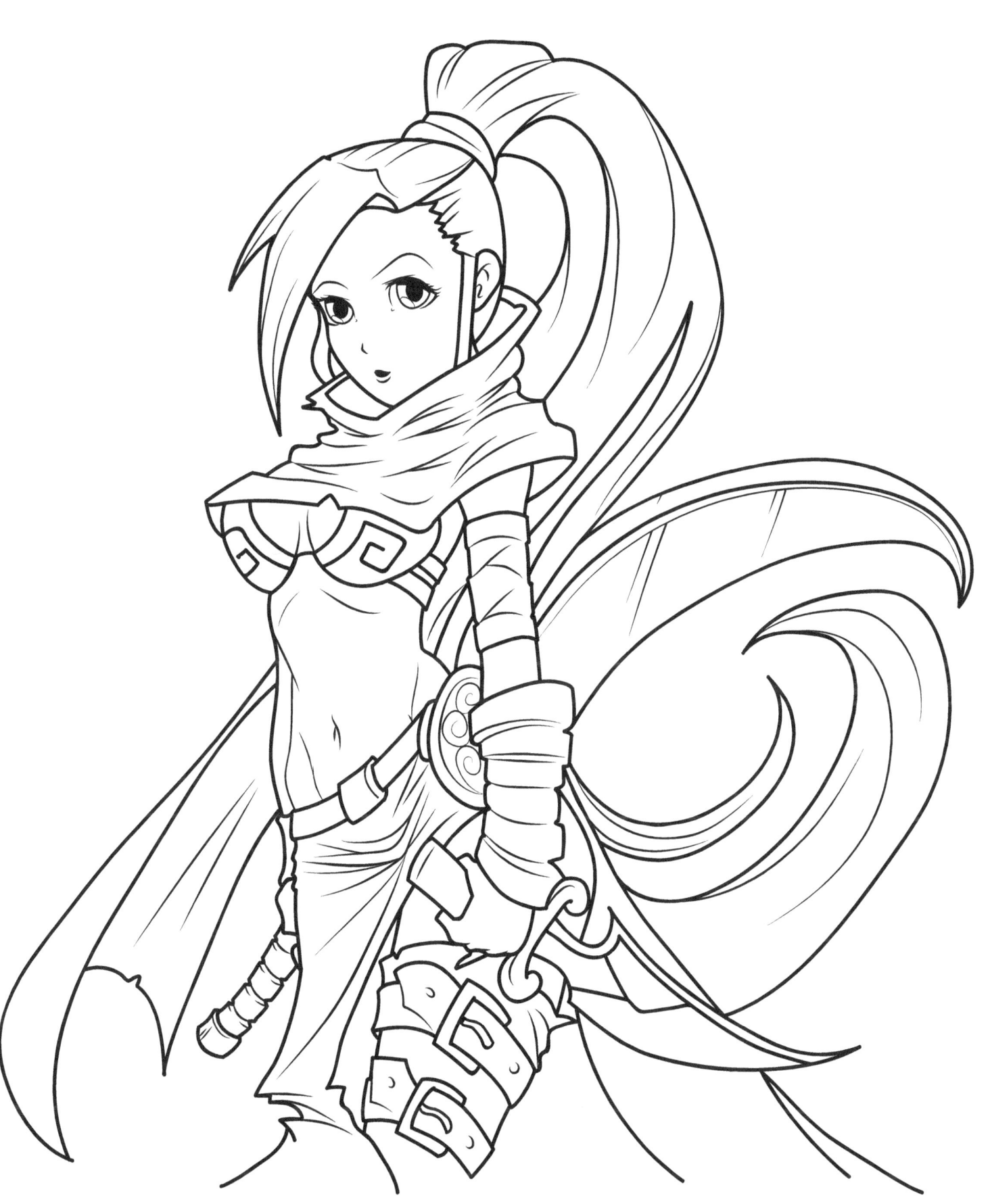

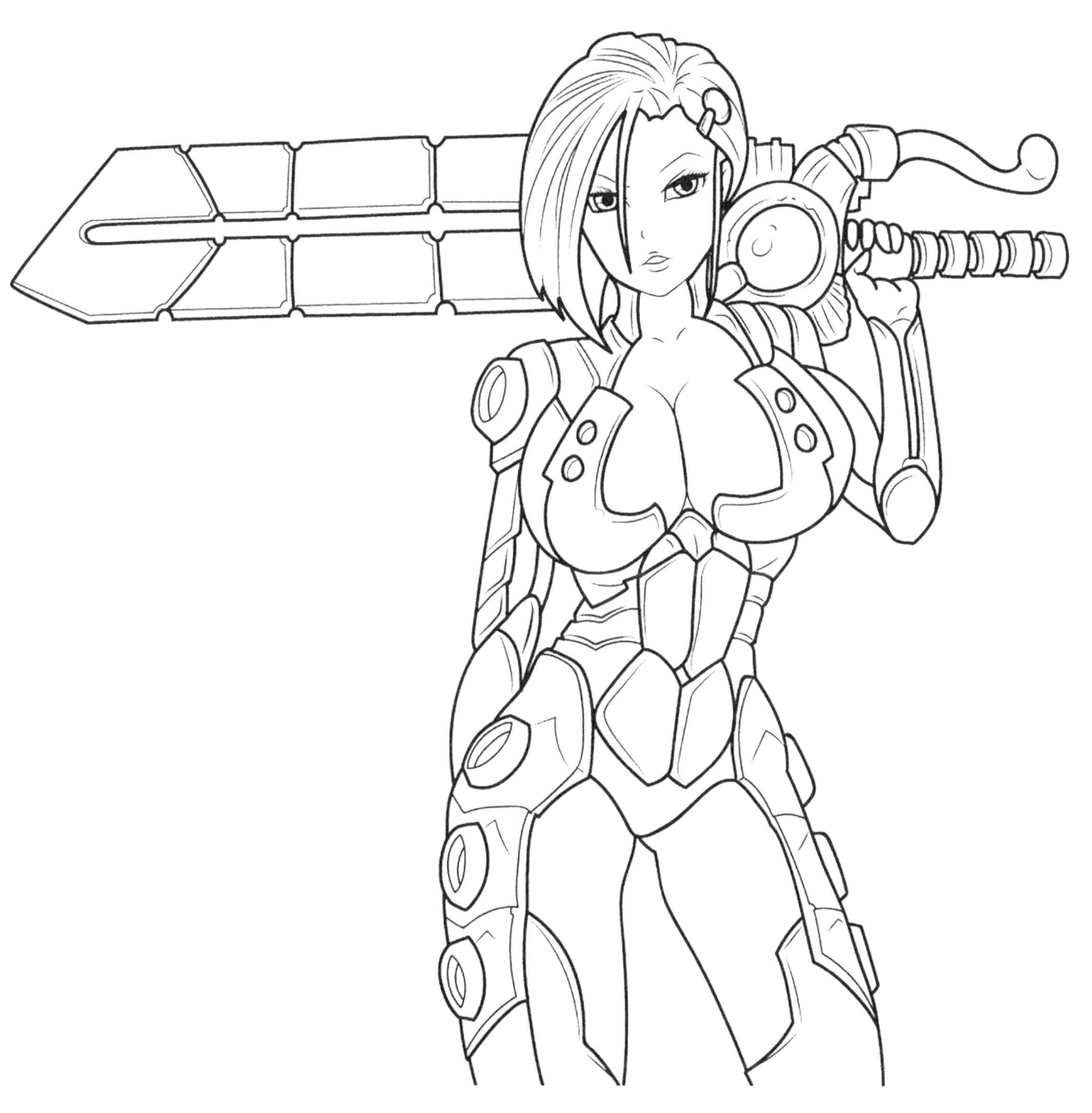

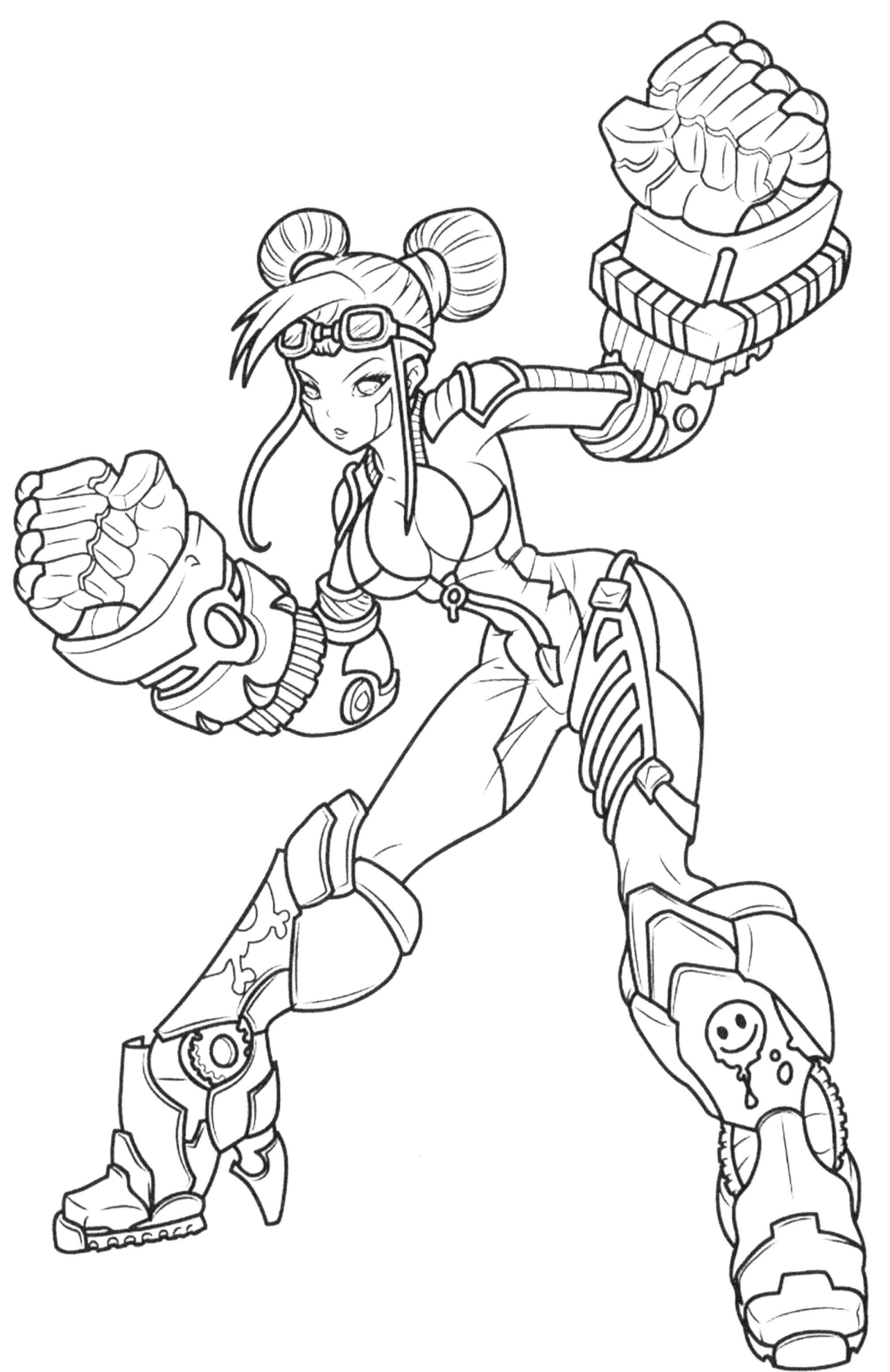

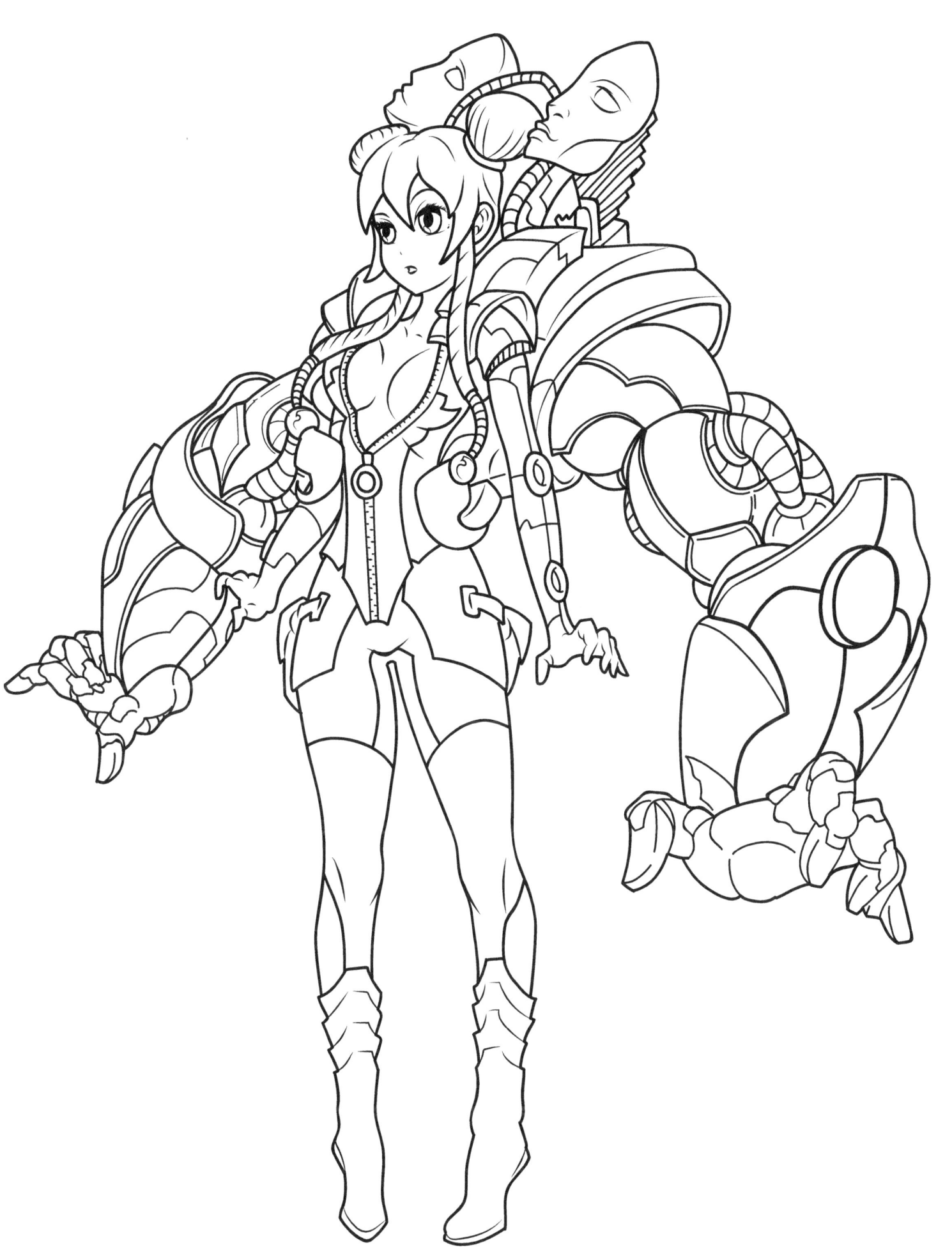

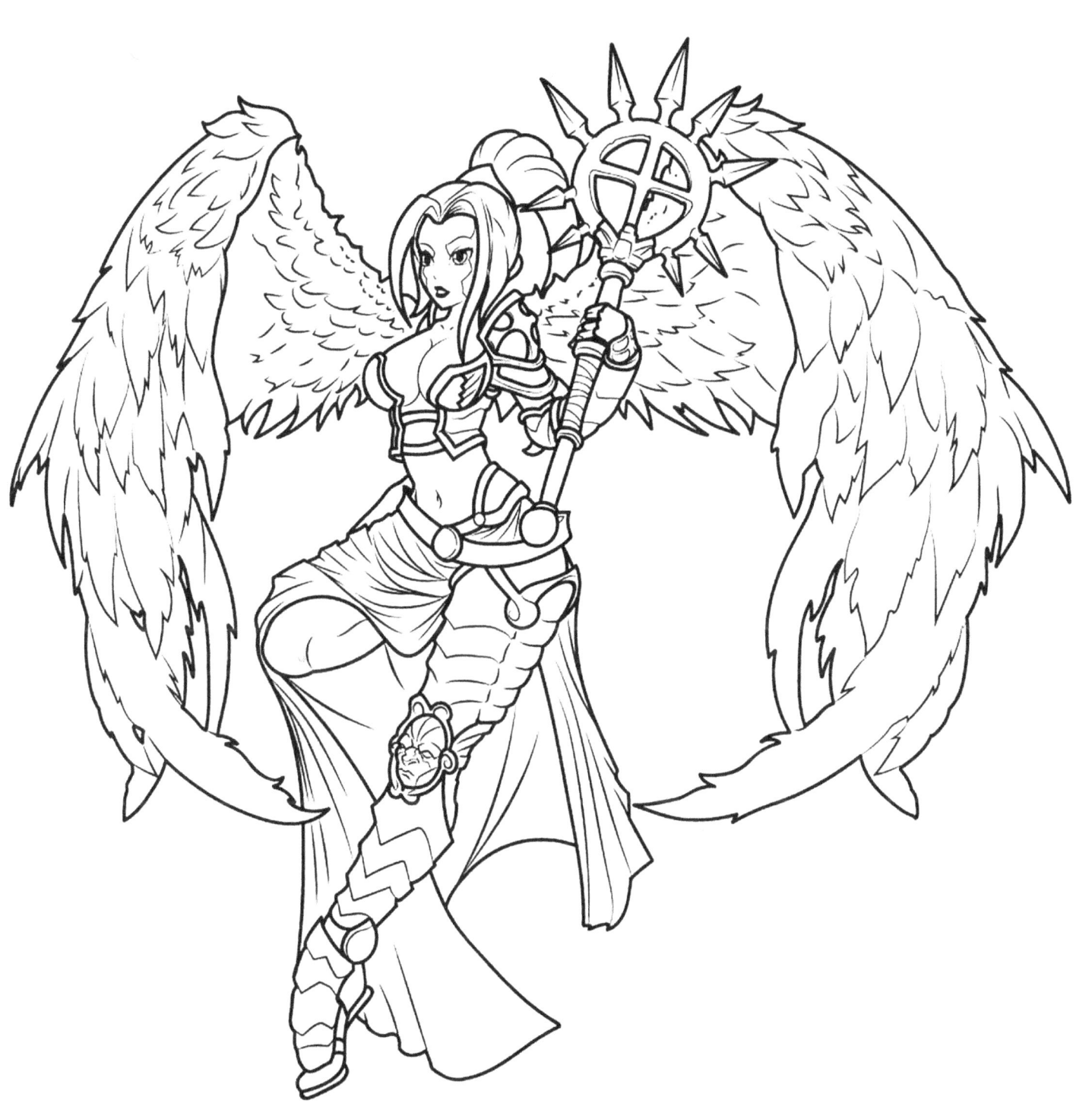

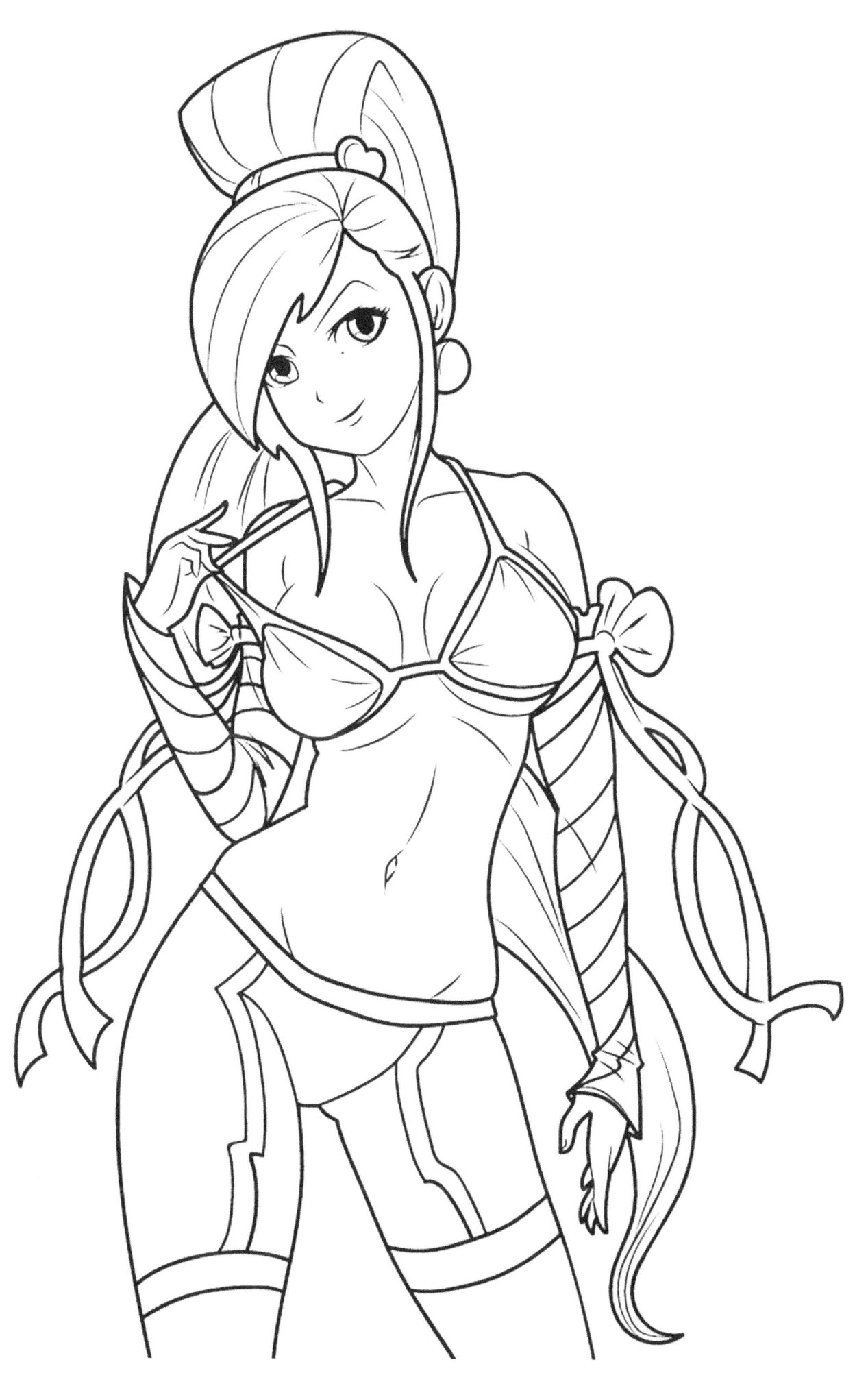

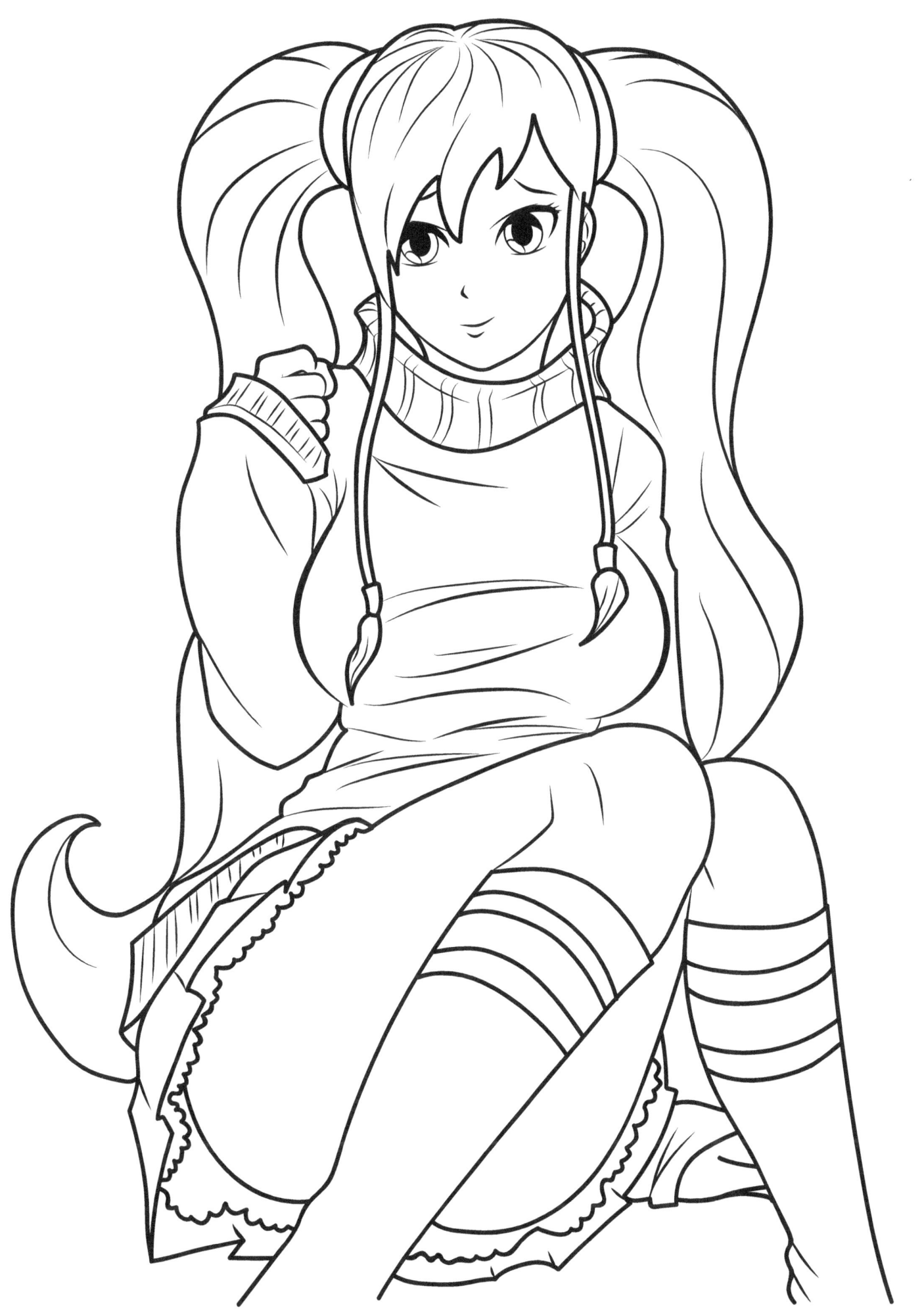

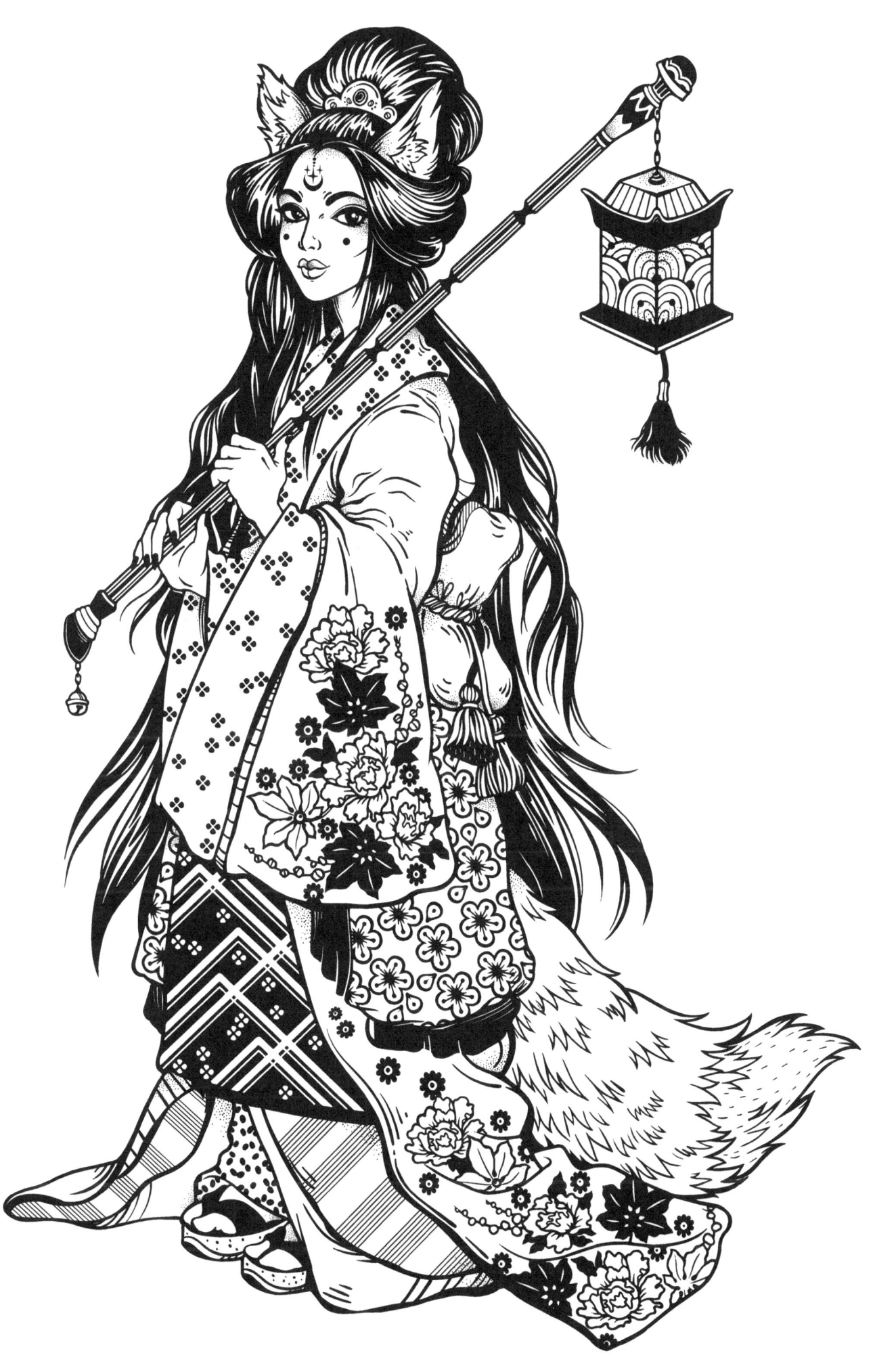

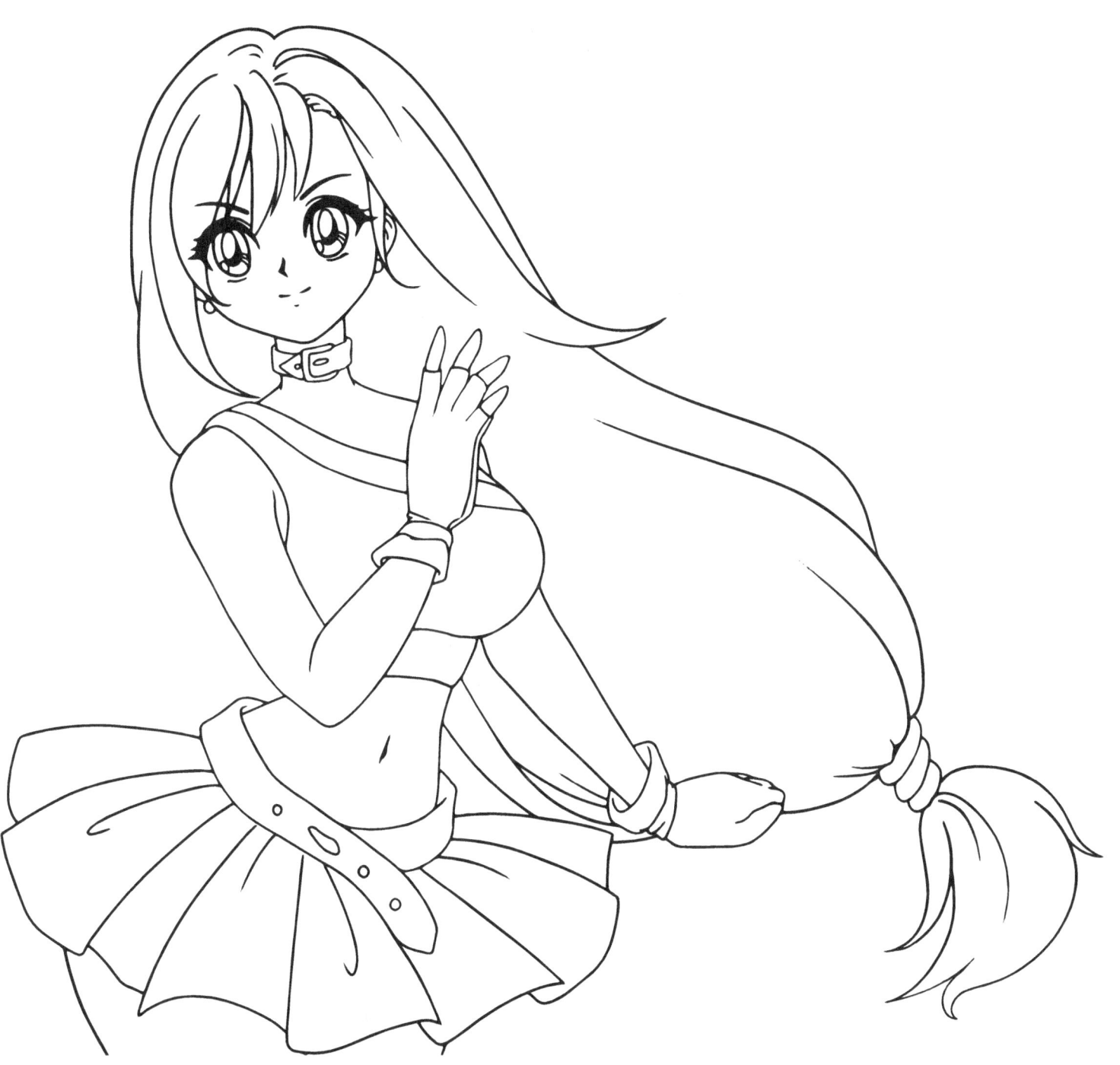

Drawing in the style of anime

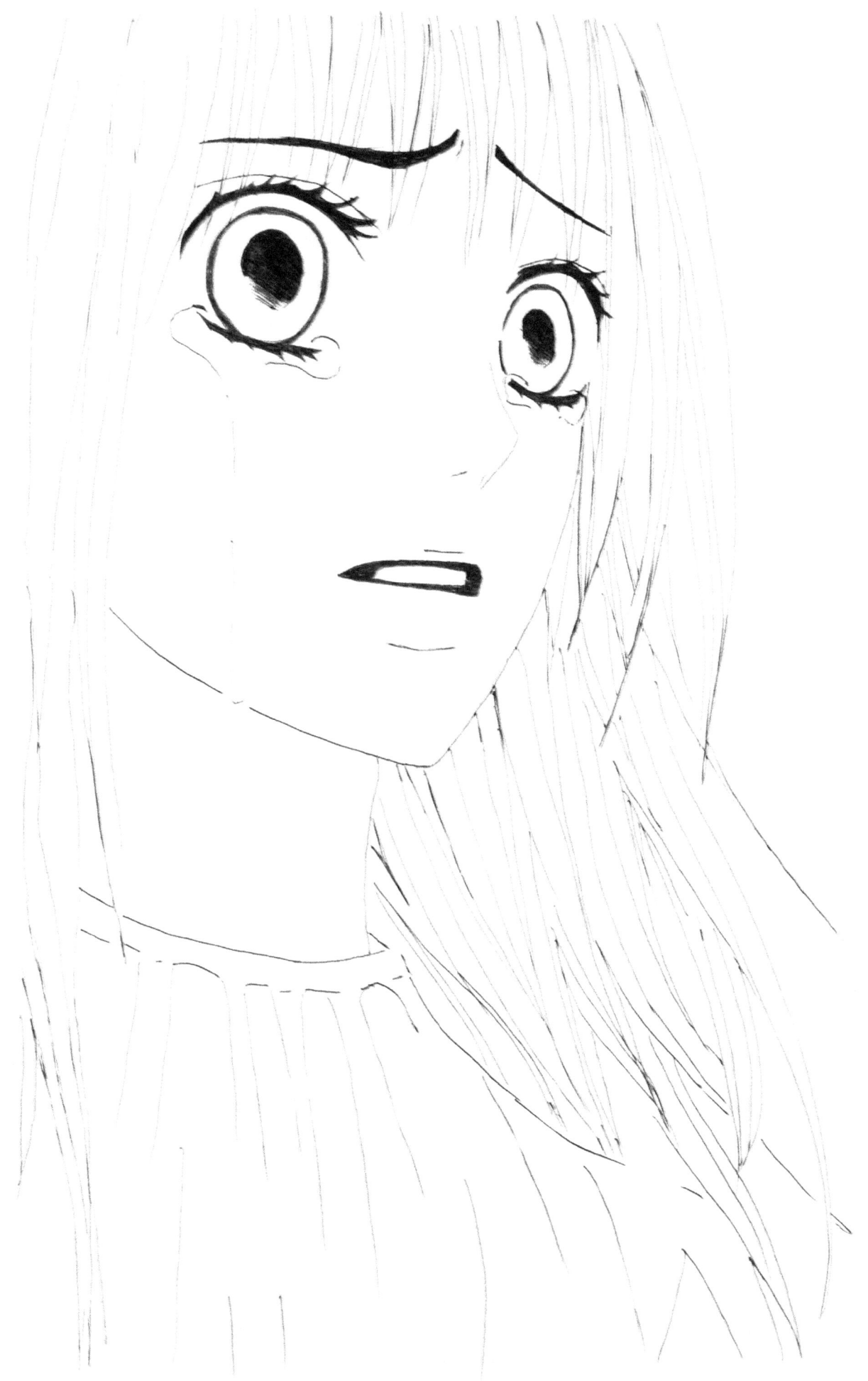

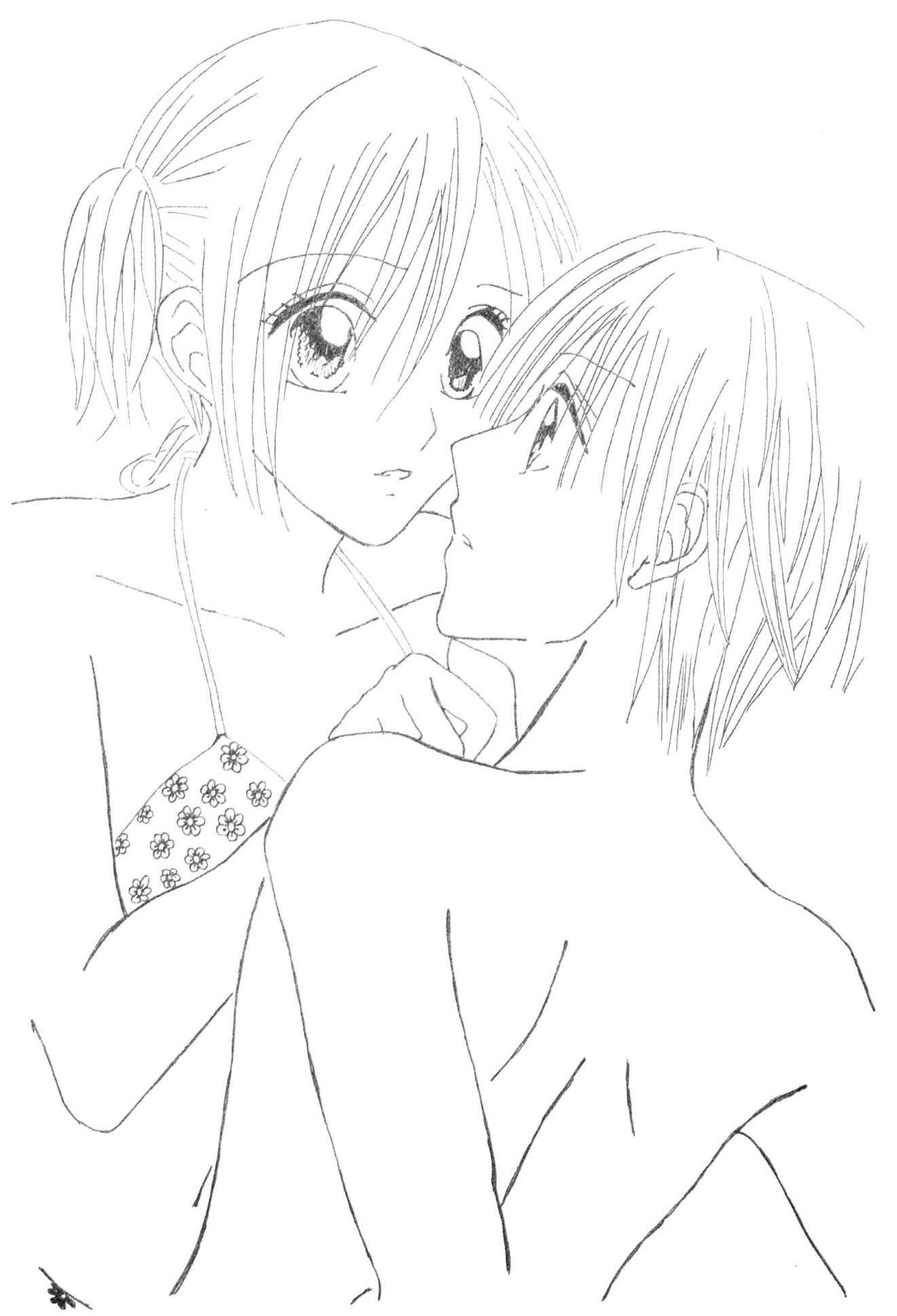

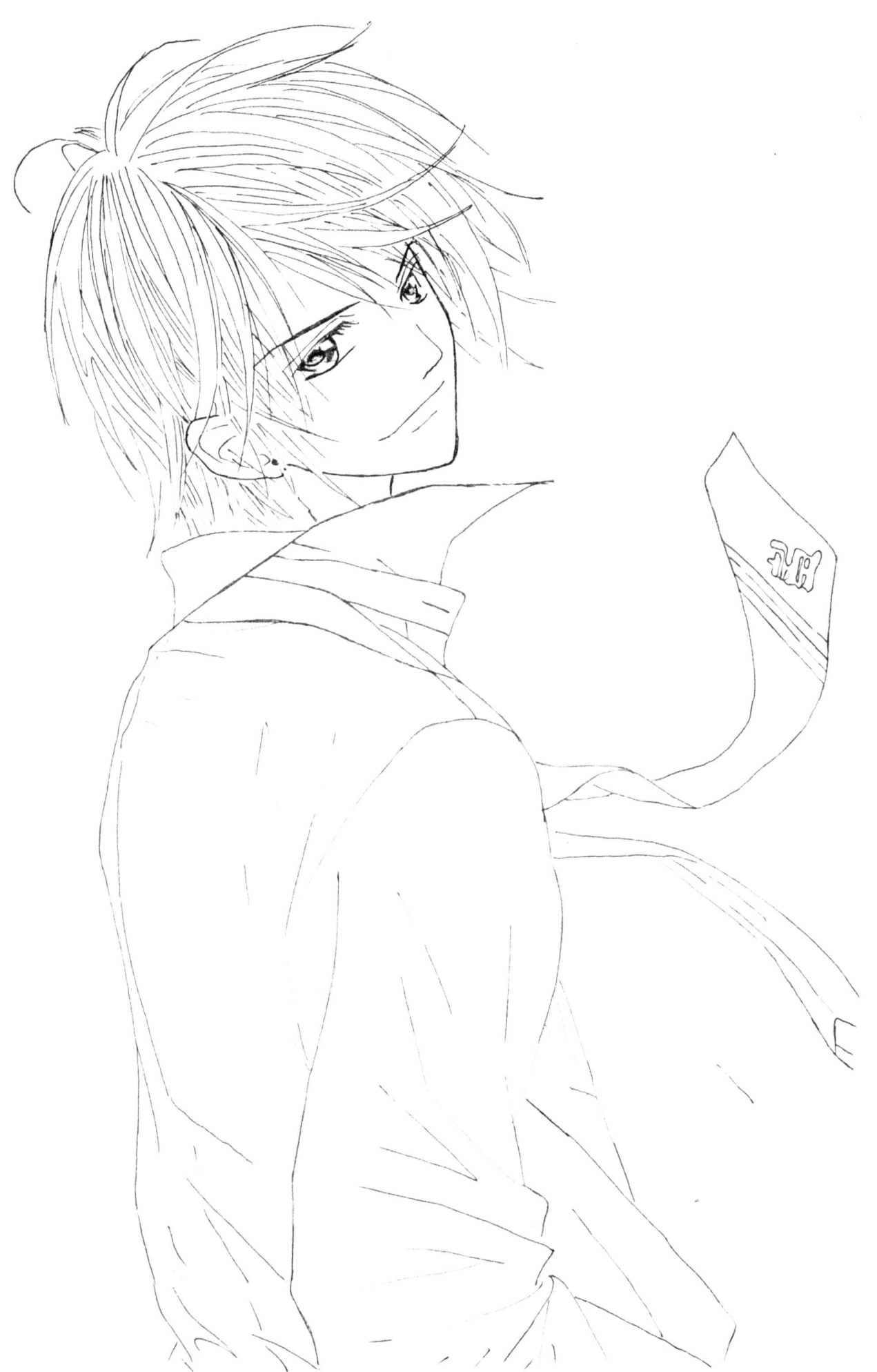

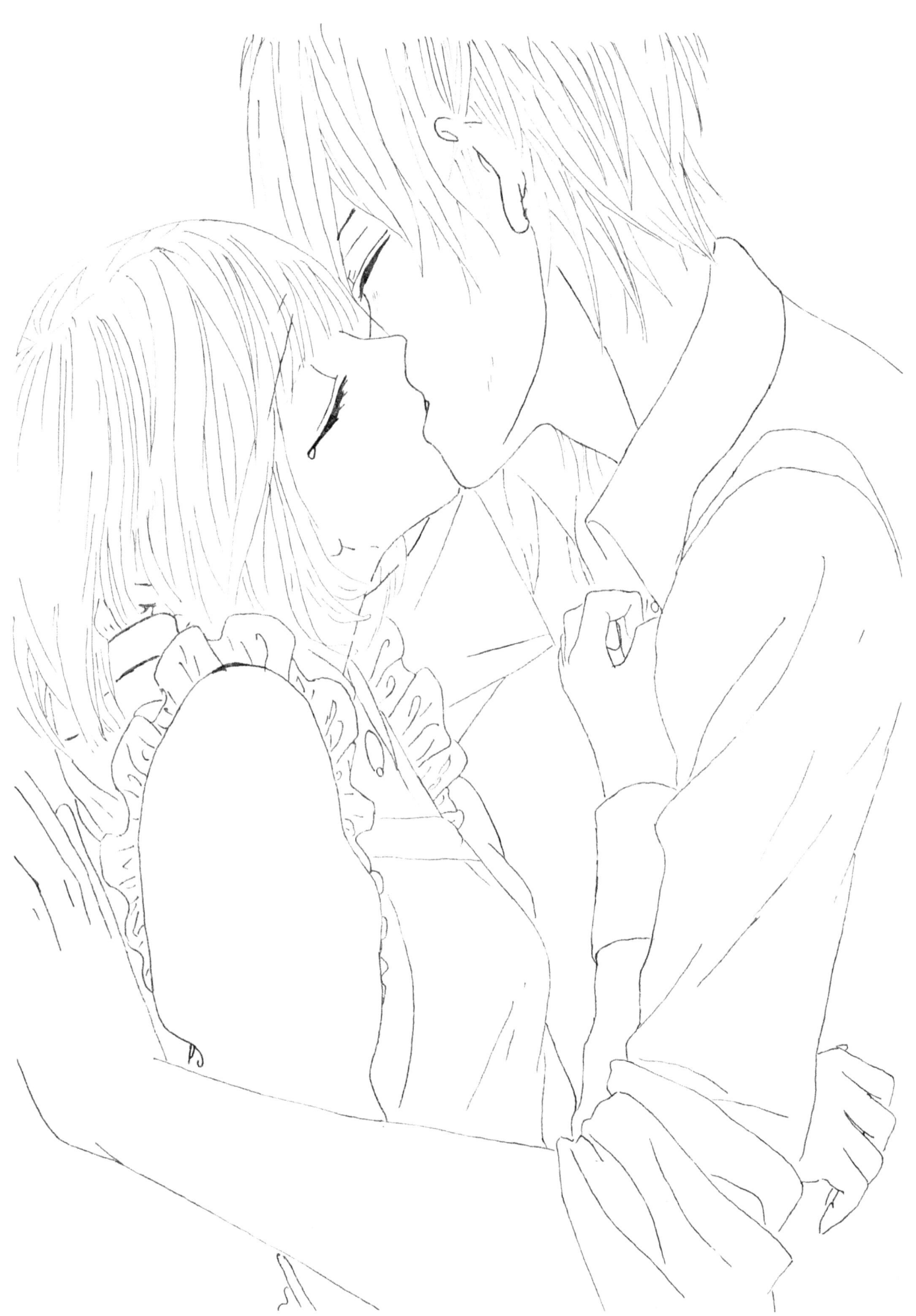

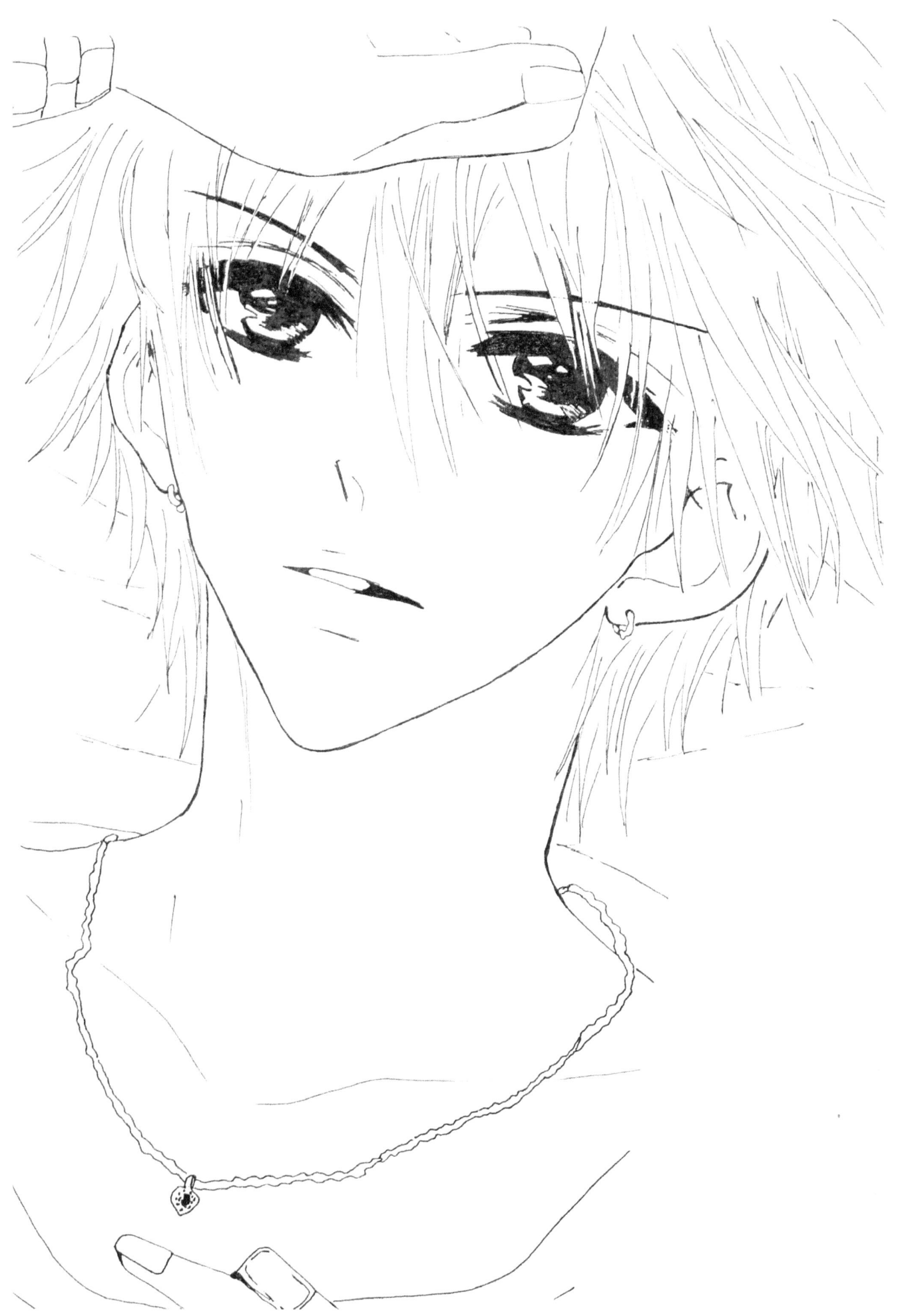

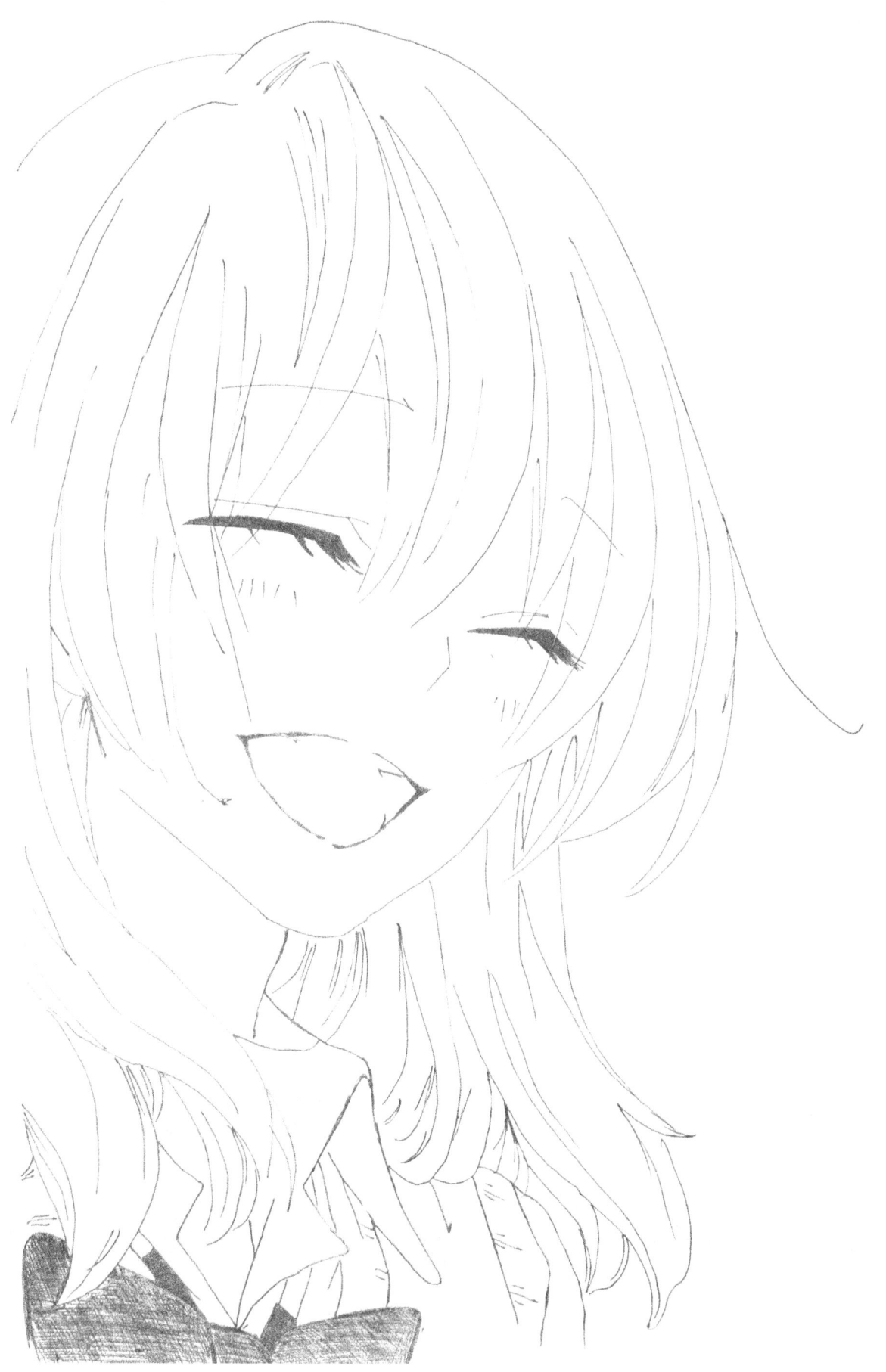

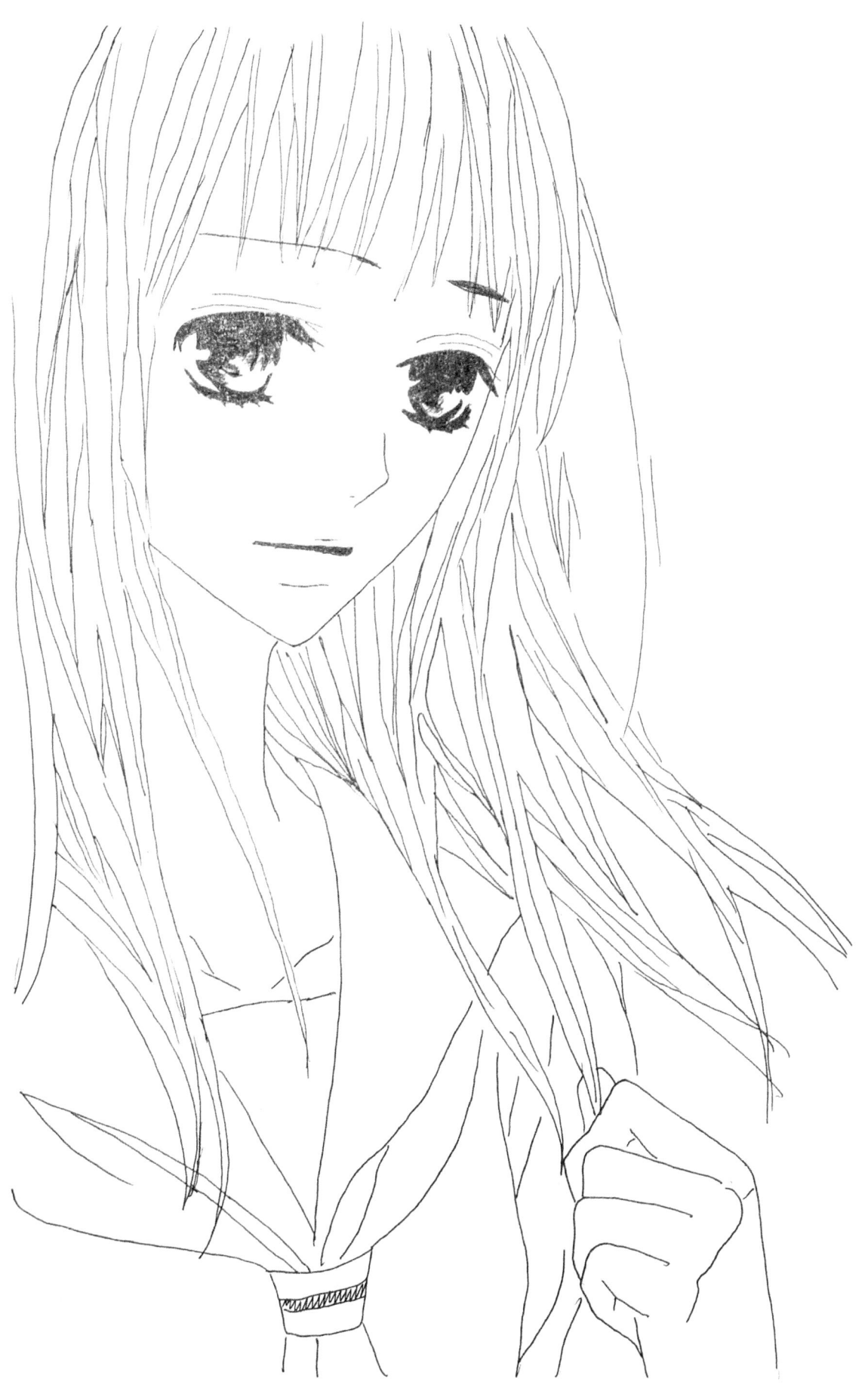

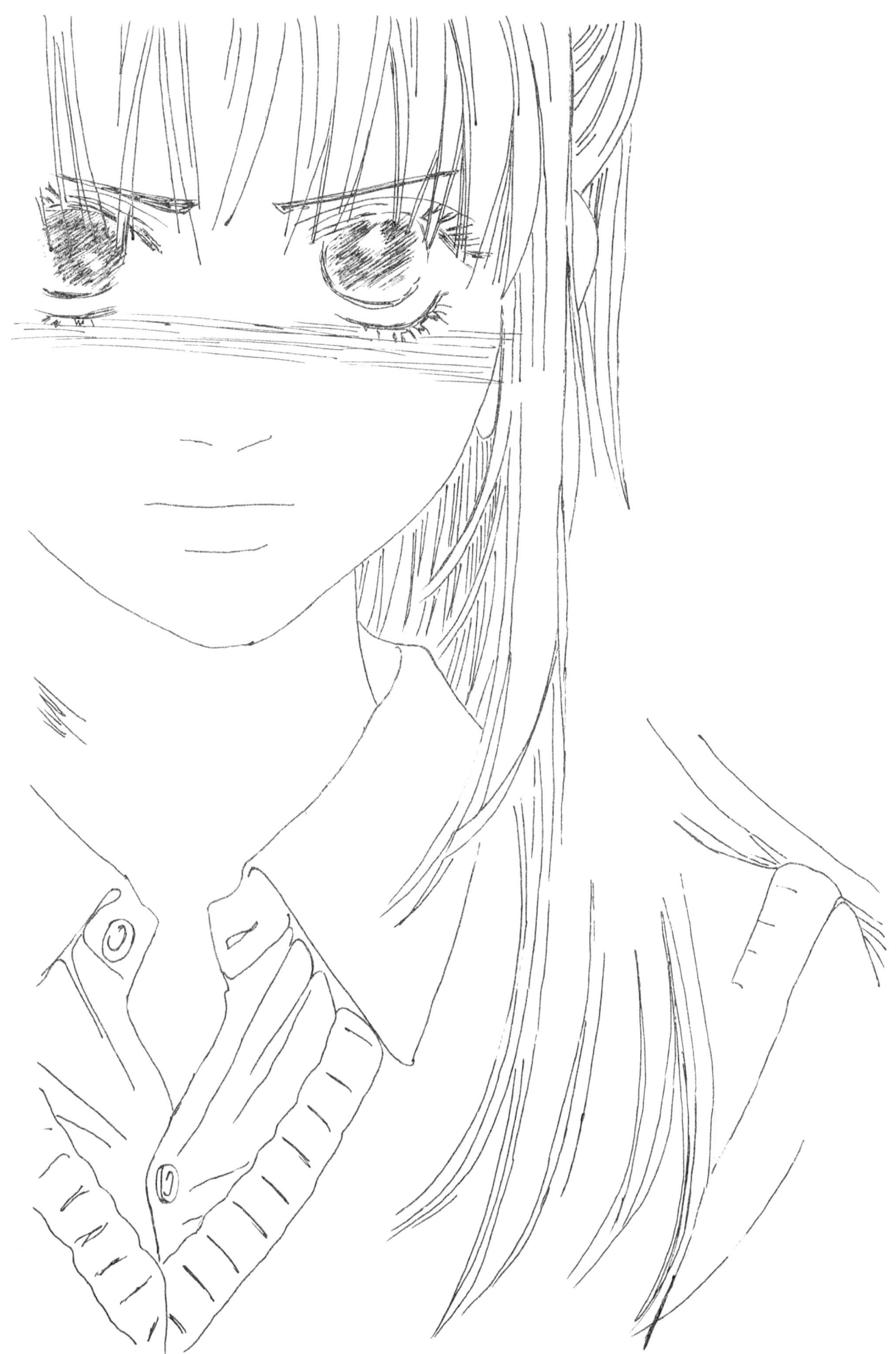

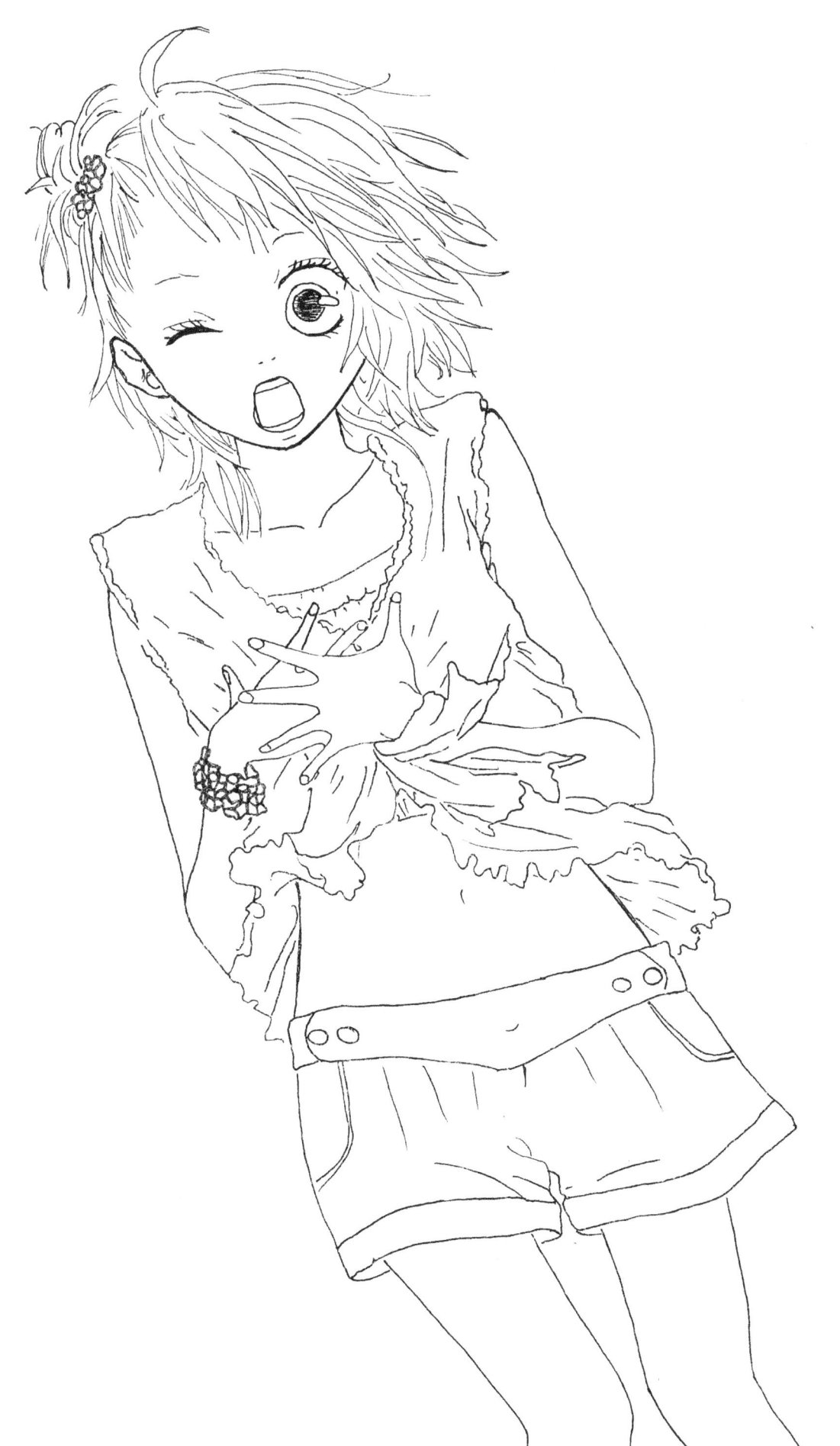

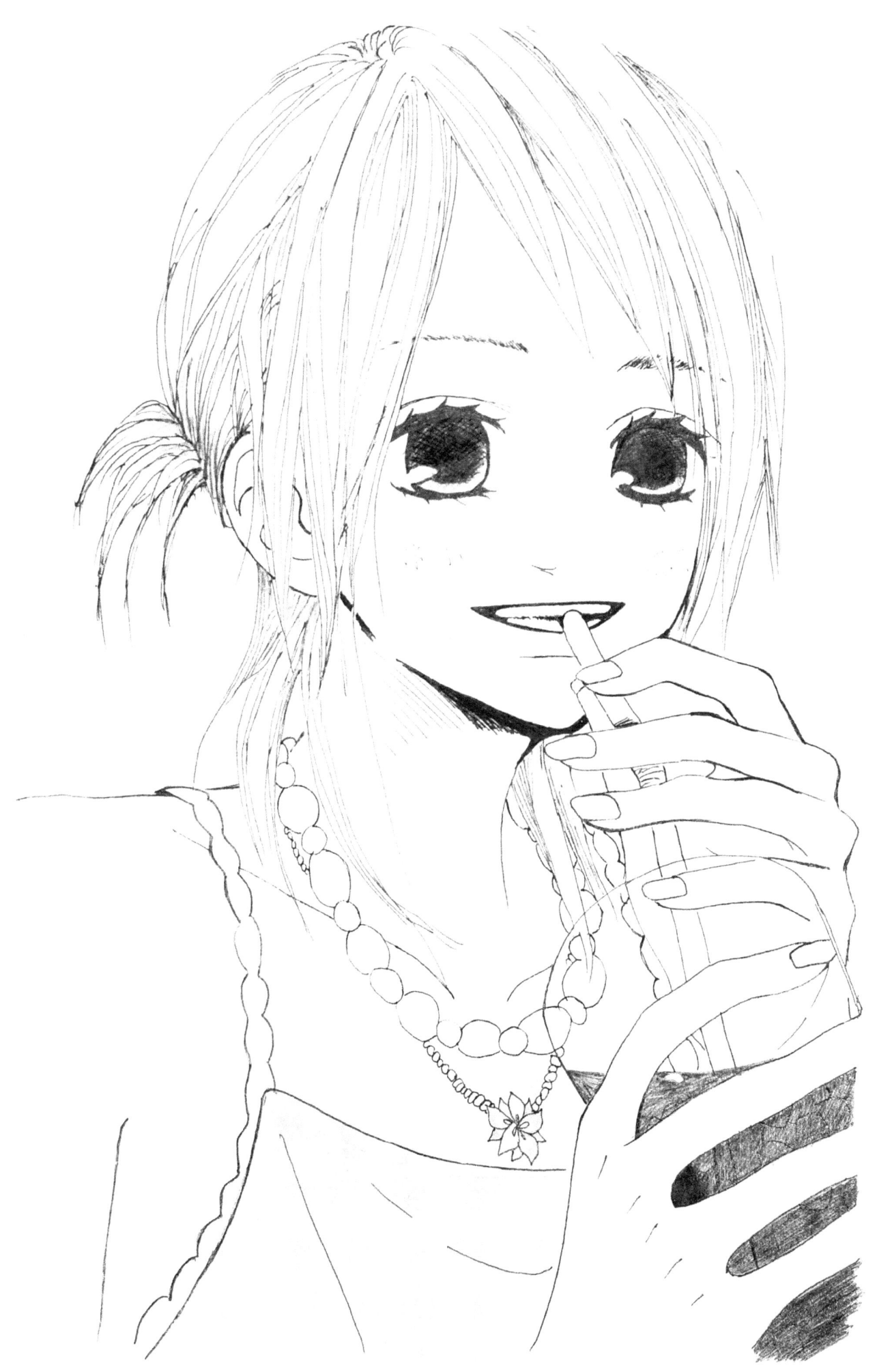

12
Zodiac
set
on
Anime

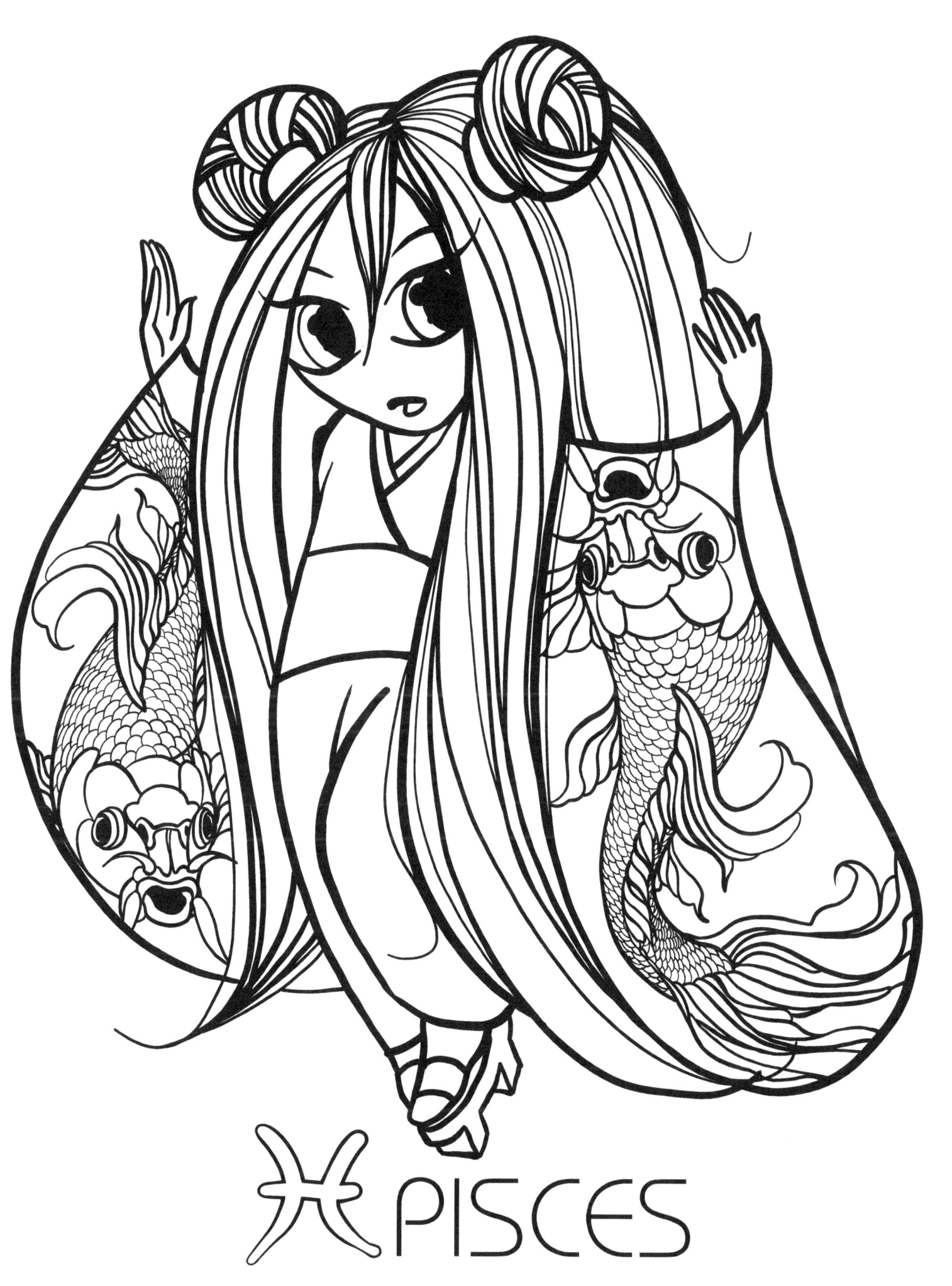

PISCES

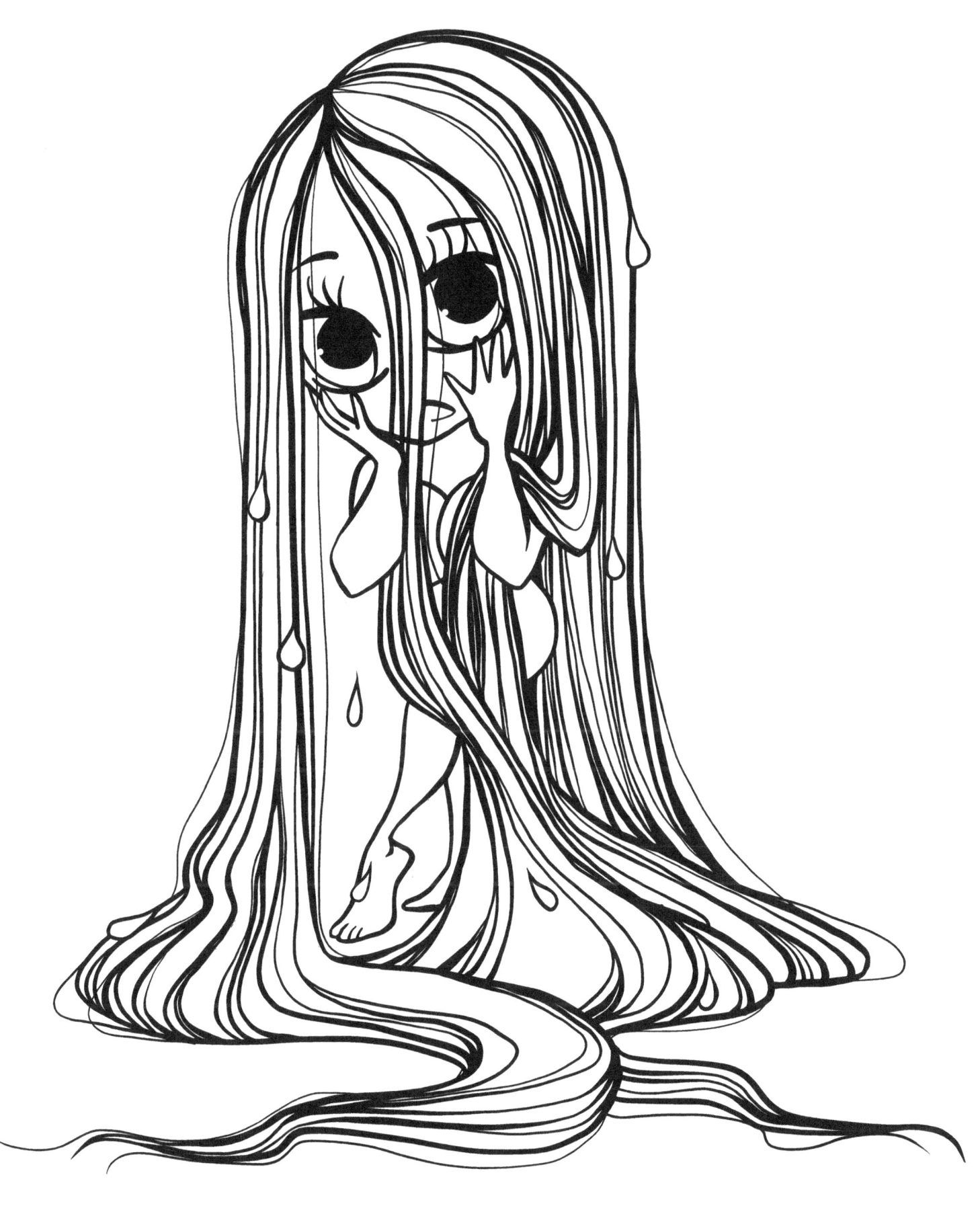

AQUARIUS

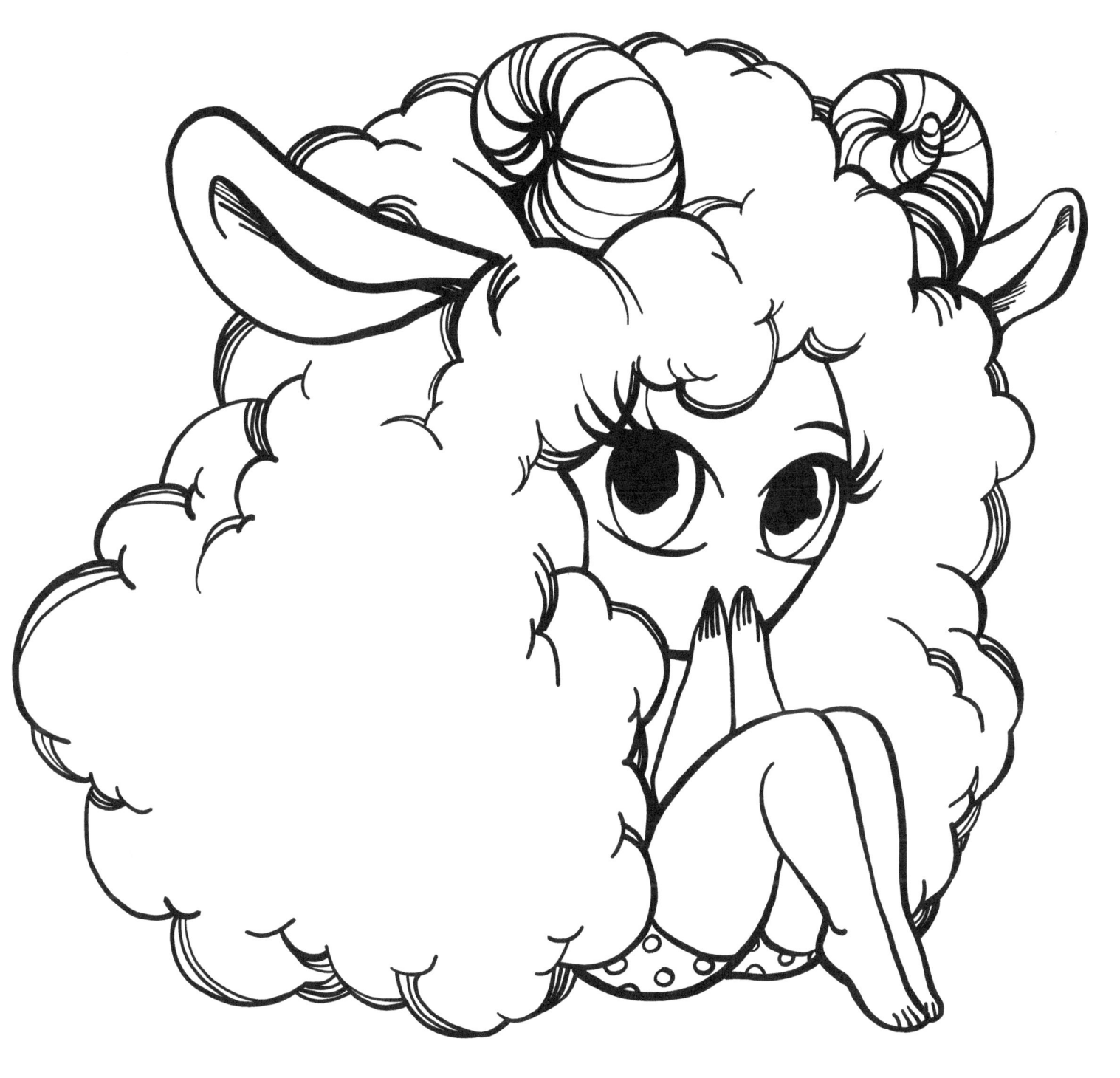

ARIES

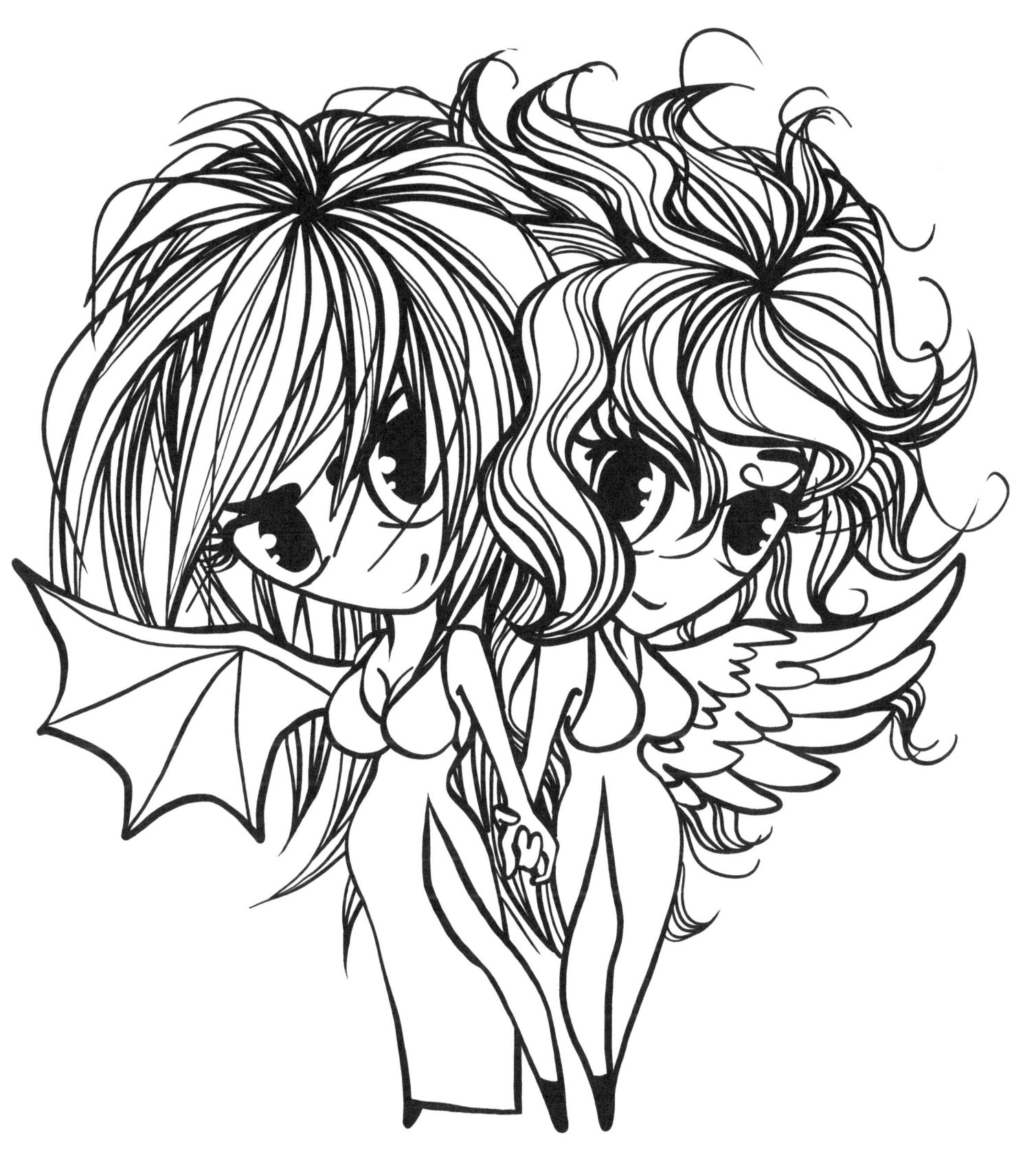

GEMINI

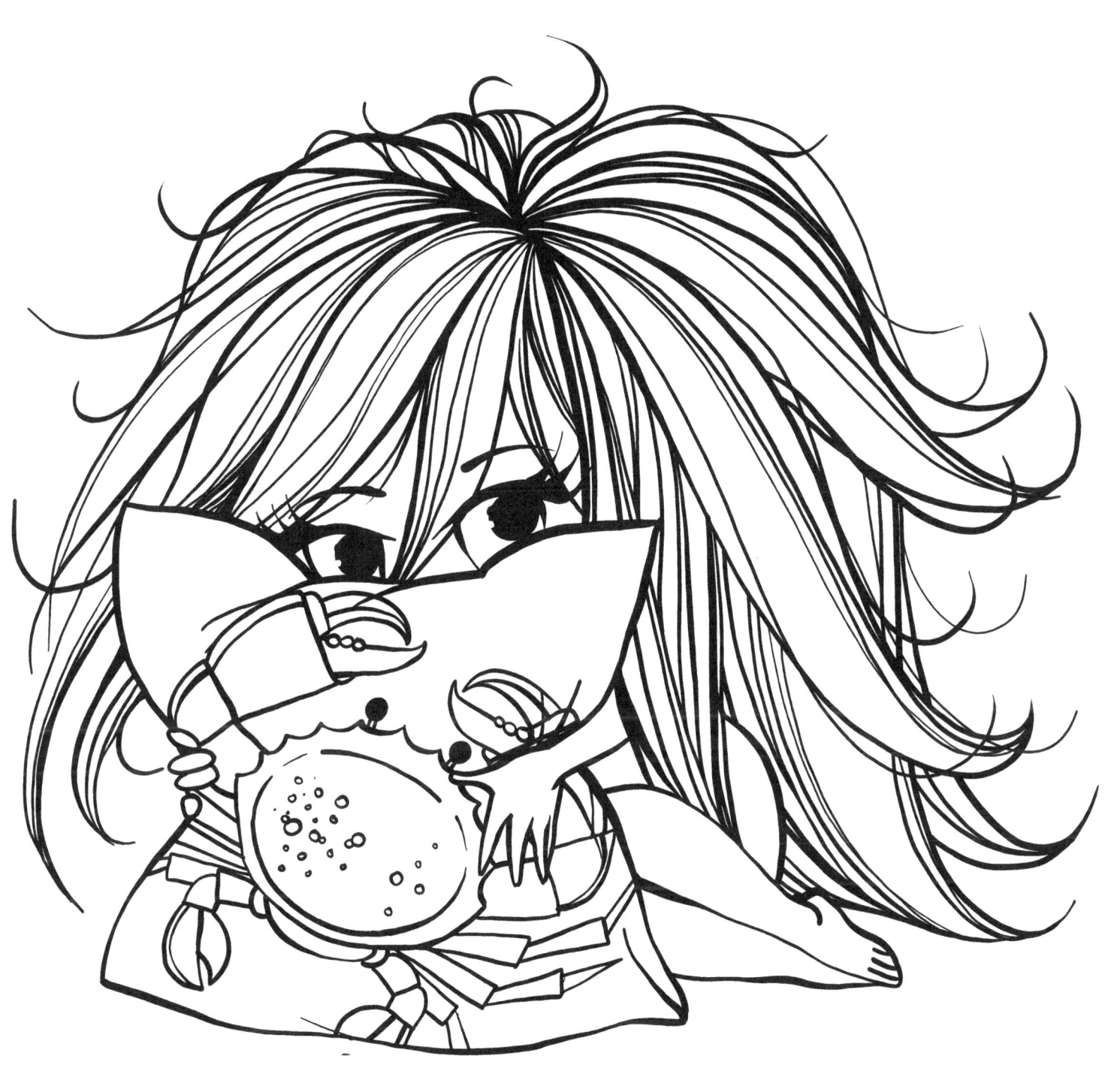

CANCER

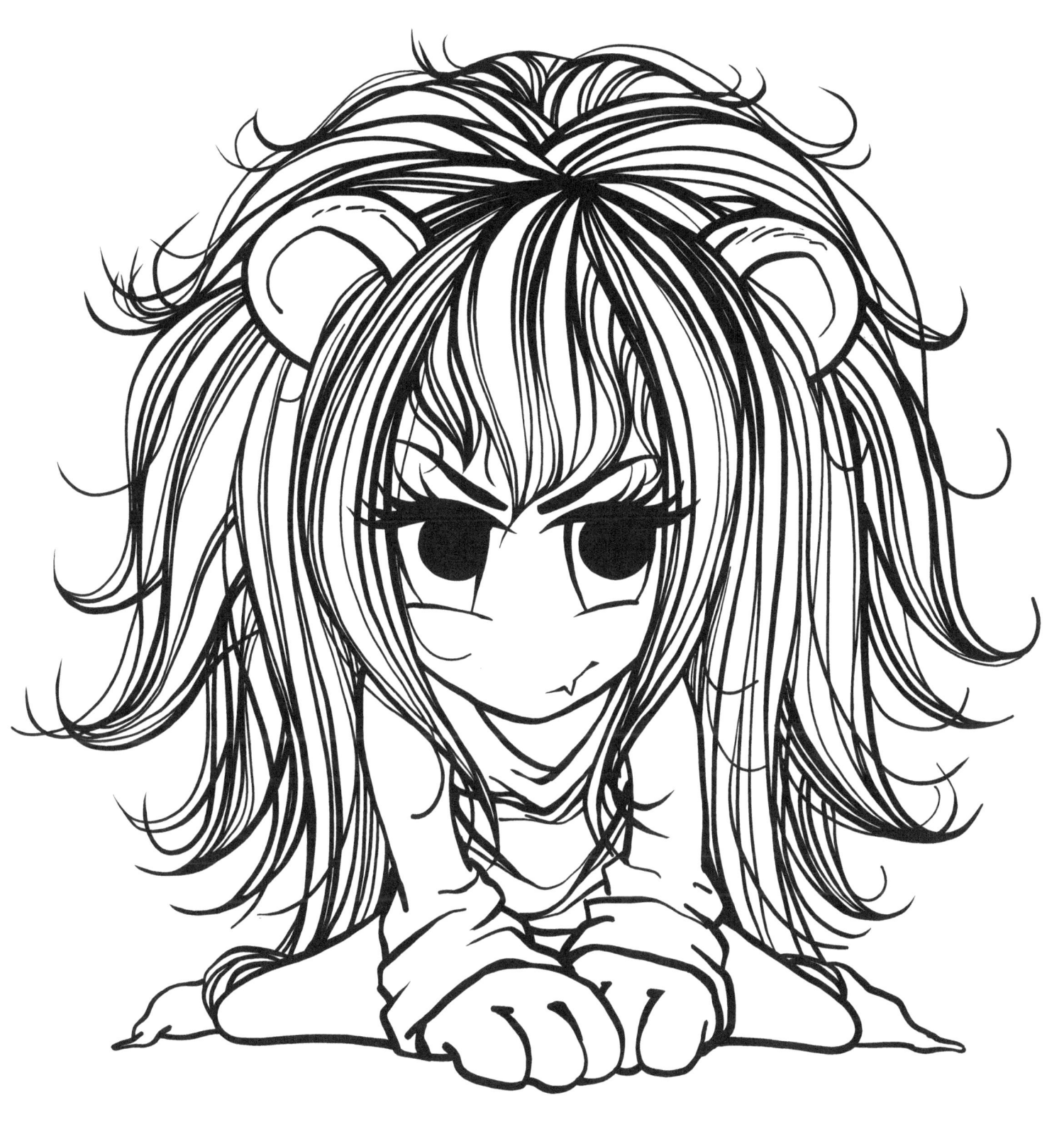

LEO

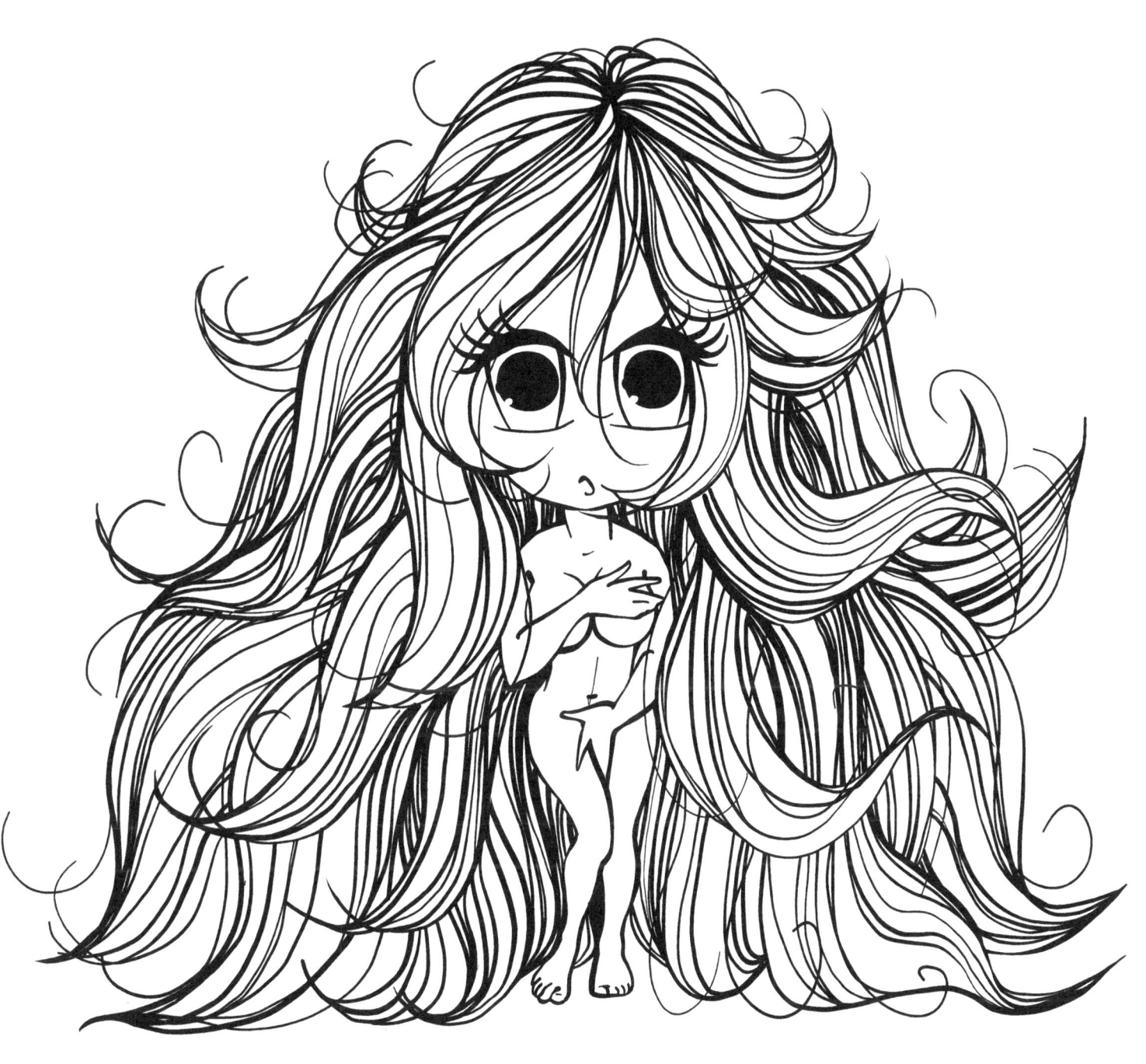

♍ VIRGO

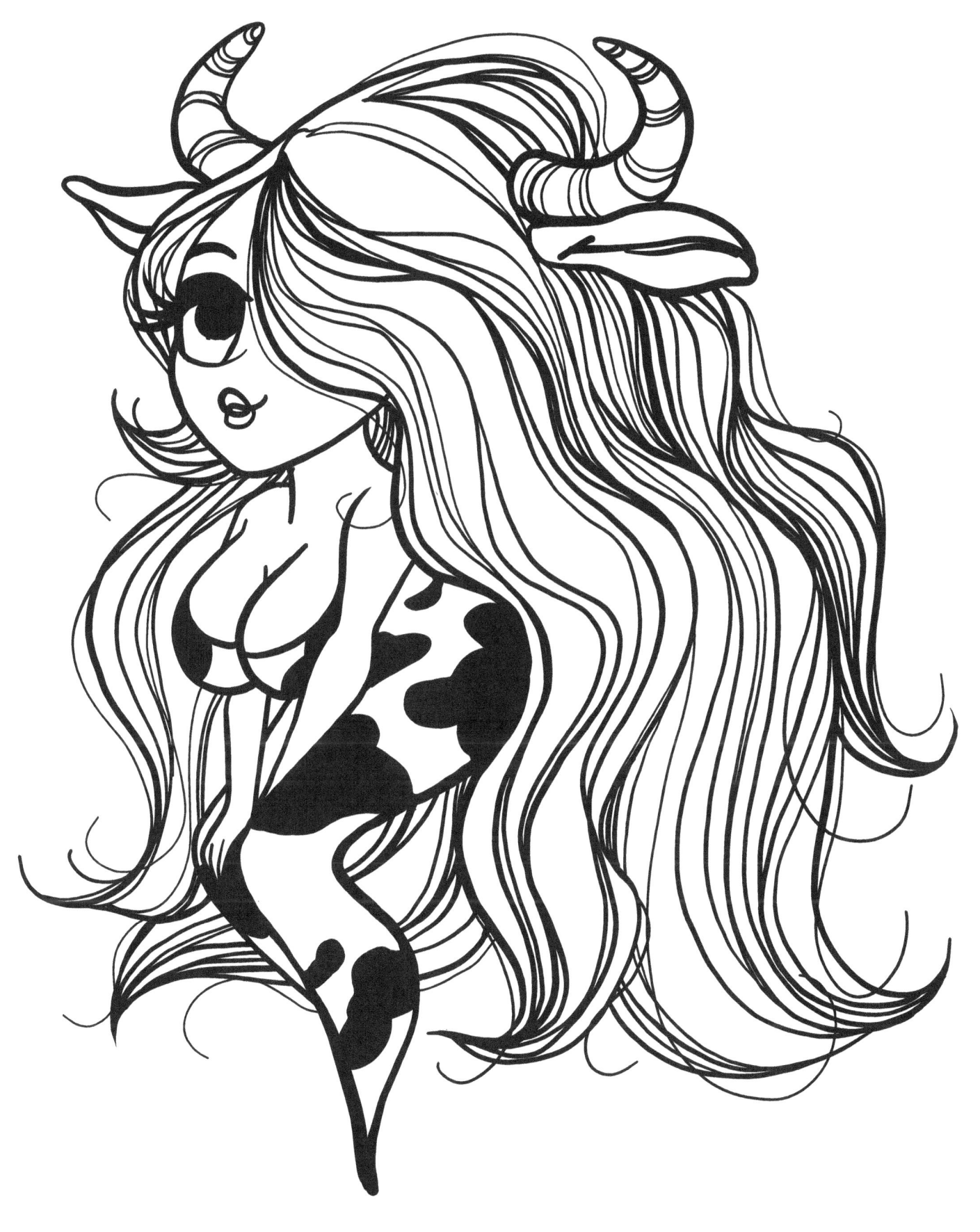

TAURUS

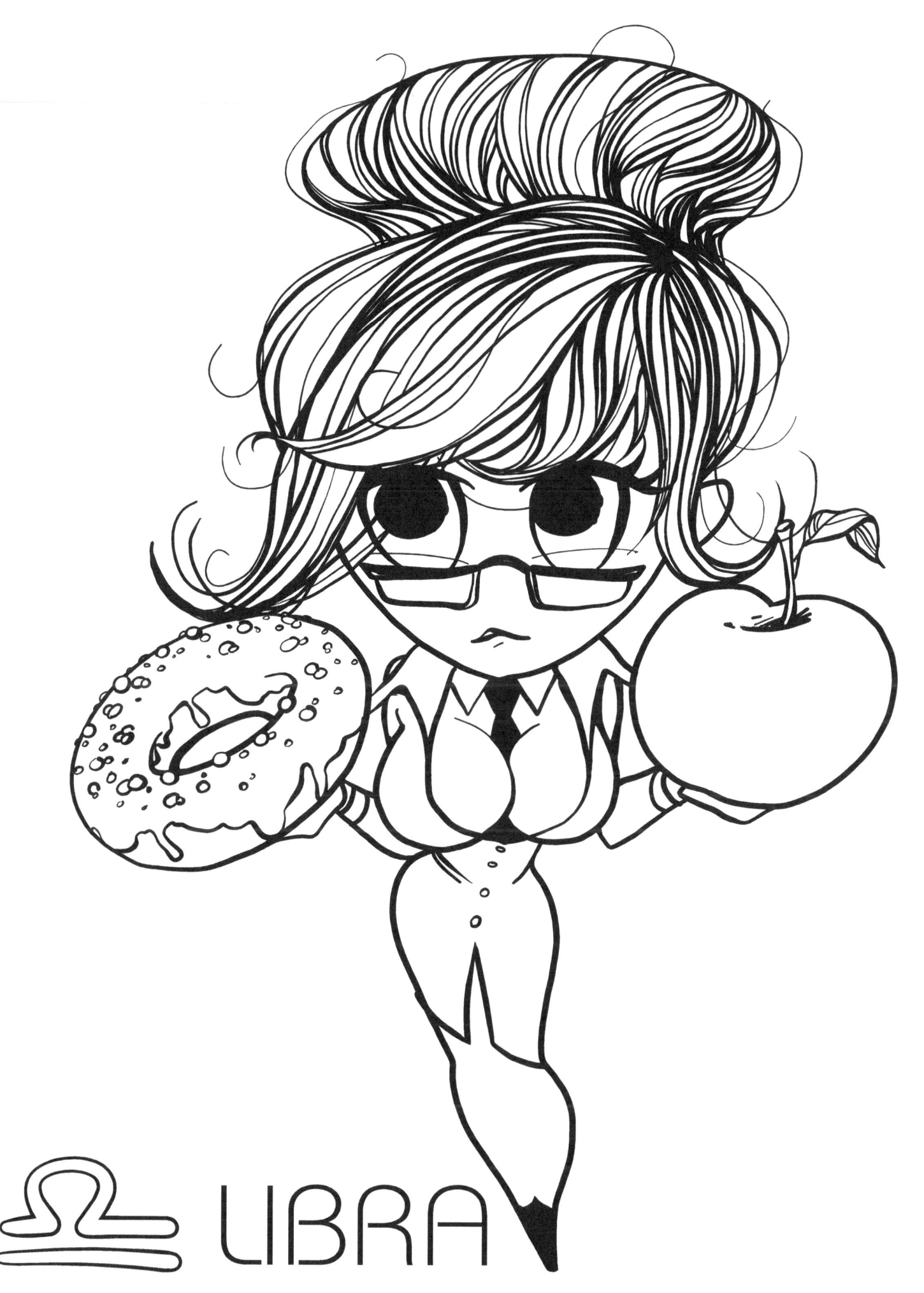

LIBRA

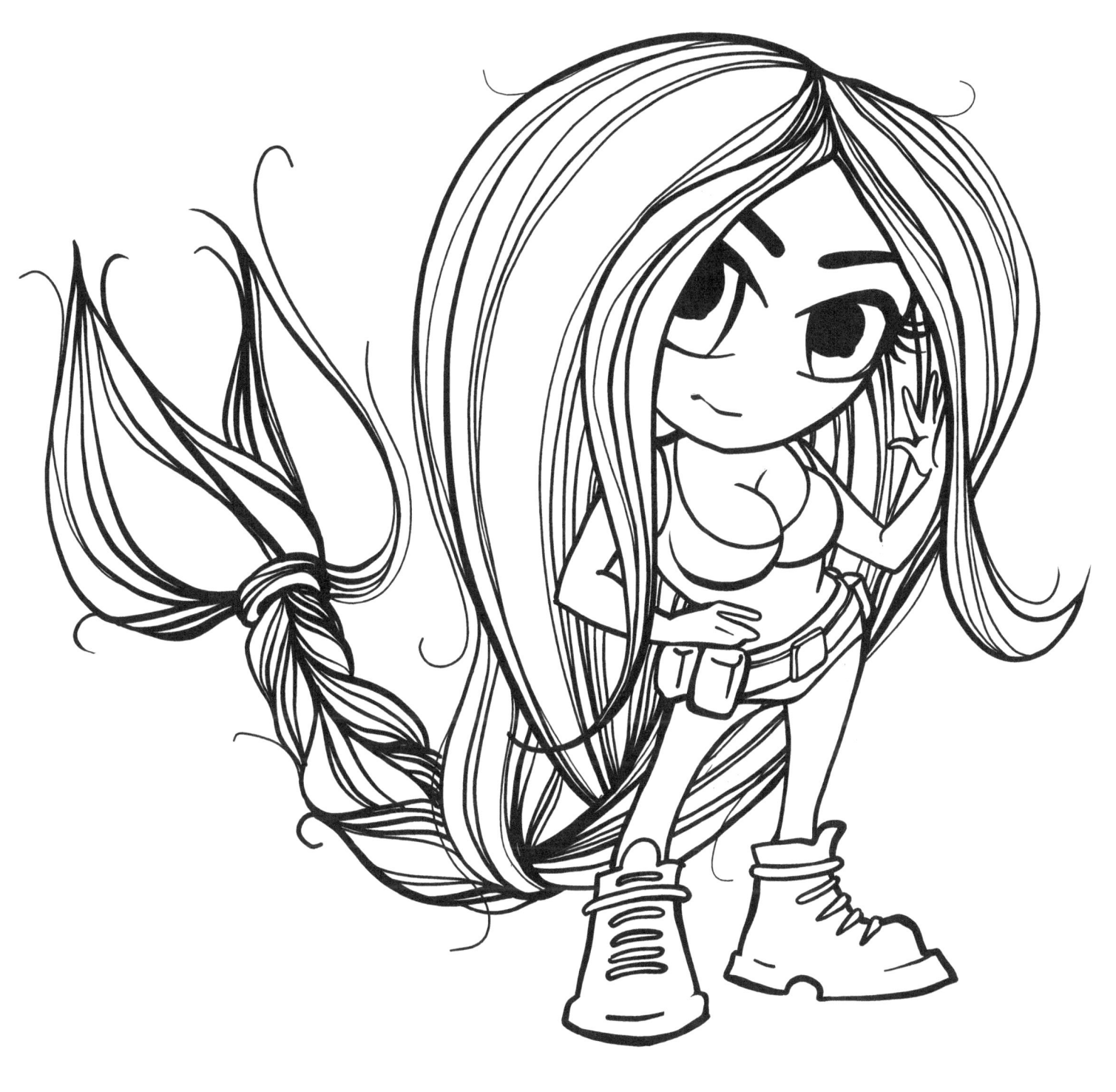

scorpio

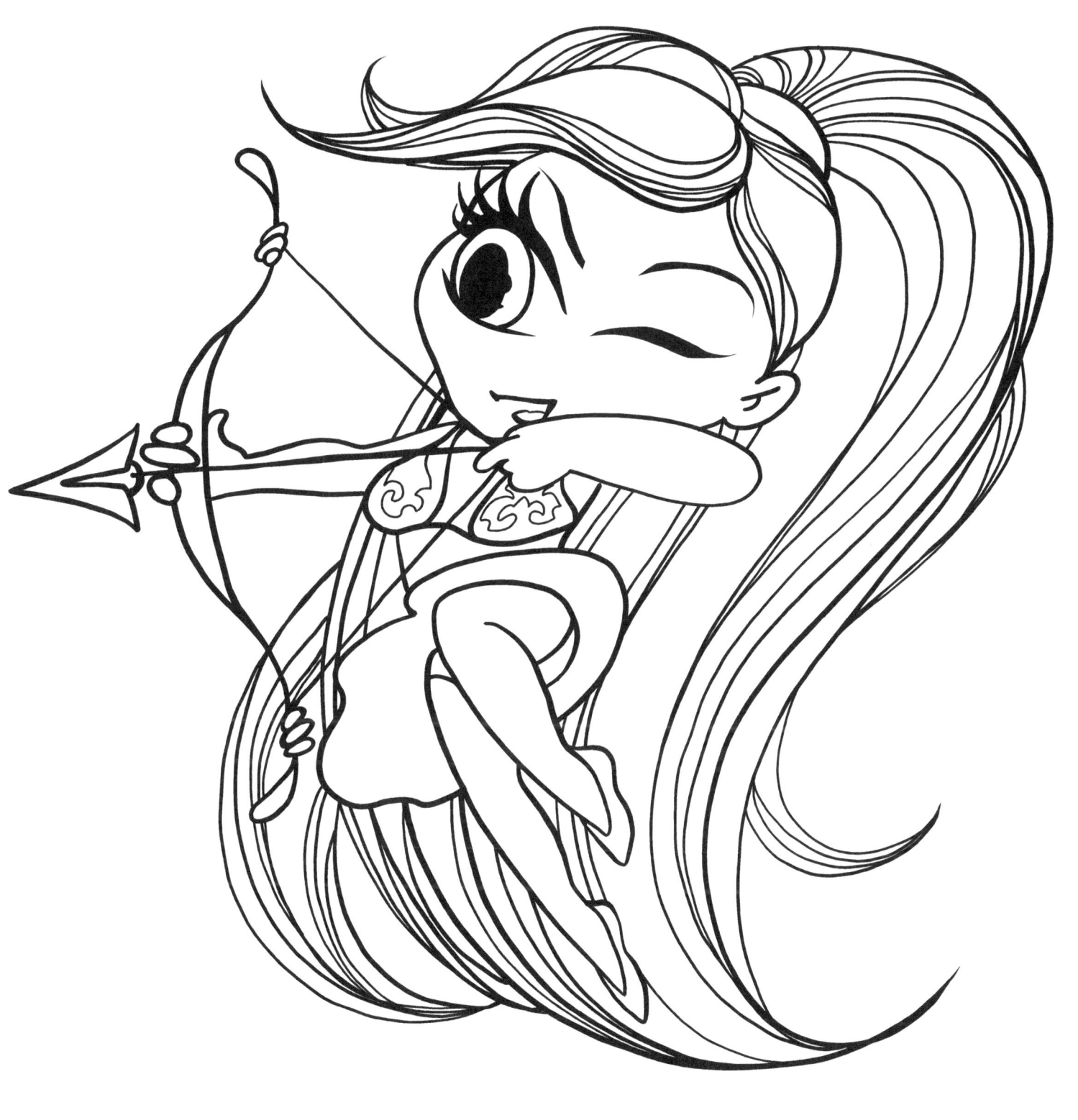

sagittarius

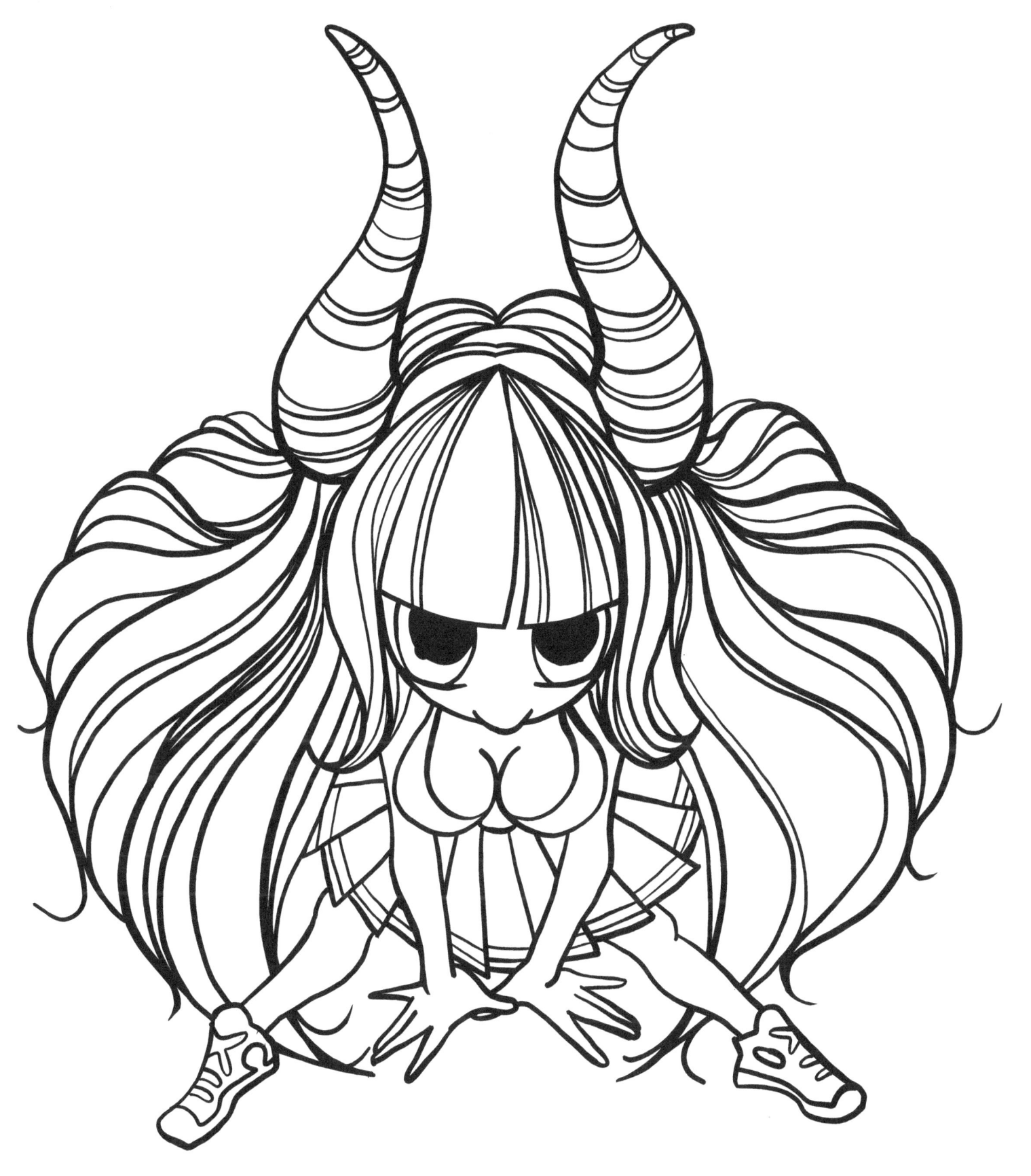

♑ CAPRICORN